THIS BOOK

BELONGS TO

....

....

Thank you for Purchasing my book and taking the time to read it from front to back. I am always grateful when a reader chooses my work and I hope you enjoyed it!

With the vast selection available online, I am touched that you chose to be purchasing my work and take valuable time out of your life to read it. My hope is that you feel you made the right decision.

I very much would like to know what you thought of the book. Please take the time to write an honest and informative review on Amazon.com. Your experience and opinions will be of great benefit to me and those readers looking to make an informed choice.

With much thanks.

Table of Contents

Introduction

Throughout our life, we all encounter a variety of emotions. I have to acknowledge that while writing this book, I went through my own highs and lows. At first, I was ecstatic and excited at the prospect of giving individuals with a guide to assist them in comprehending their feelings. I thought how much better readers' lives would be if they could control their emotions. My motivation was strong, and I couldn't stop myself from fantasizing about how fantastic the book would be.

Or so I reasoned.

After the initial thrill worn off, the time came to settle down and write the real book, and the excitement swiftly faded off. Suddenly, concepts that were brilliant in my head appeared mundane. My writing was tedious, and I felt as though I had anything significant or worthwhile to add.

Each day, sitting at my desk and writing got increasingly difficult. I began to lose confidence. Who was I to write a book on emotions if I was incapable of mastering my own? What irony! I pondered quitting. There are already enough books on the subject, so why add another?

Simultaneously, I saw that this book provided an ideal chance to work on my emotional difficulties. And who doesn't experience bad feelings on occasion? We all have ups and downs, don't we? The critical factor is how we respond to our lows. Are we using our emotions to help us grow and learn, or are we punishing ourselves for them?

Therefore, let us now discuss your feelings. Let me begin by asking you how you are feeling right now.

Understanding your emotions is the first step in gaining control of them. You may have internalized so much that you've lost touch with your emotions. Perhaps you said, "I believe this book may be beneficial," or "I believe I may learn something from this book."

None of these responses, however, reflect how you feel. You do not 'feel this way or that way,' you simply 'feel.' You don't 'feel like' this book may be beneficial; you 'believe' it might be valuable, which creates an emotion that makes you 'feel' eager about reading it. Feelings are real feelings in your body, not mental concepts. Perhaps the reason the term 'feel' is so often overused or abused is because we are averse to discussing our feelings.

How are you feeling now?

Why is it necessary to discuss emotions?

Your emotional state dictates the quality of your life. Your emotions may either make or break your life. That is why they are among the most critical areas to concentrate on. All of your experiences are colored by your emotions. When you are in a positive state of mind, everything seems, feels, and tastes better. Additionally, you think more clearly. Your vitality is increased, and opportunities appear unlimited.

On the other hand, when you are melancholy, everything seems boring. You lack energy and become demotivated. You feel trapped (mentally and physically) in a place you don't want to be, and the future seems bleak.

Additionally, your emotions might serve as an effective guide. They may alert you to problems and enable you to make necessary adjustments in your life. As such, they may be among your most effective personal development tools.

Regrettably, neither your instructors nor your parents taught you how to understand or regulate your emotions. I find it strange that almost everything comes with an instruction manual, but your mind does not. Have you ever gotten a guidebook explaining how your mind works and how to utilize it to better regulate your emotions? I have not done so. Indeed, until recently, I had doubts that one existed at all.

This is the instruction handbook your parents should have given you at your birth. It's the guidebook you should have gotten in elementary school. I'll cover all you need to know about emotions in order to overcome your fears and limits and develop into the sort of person you want.

More precisely, this book will assist you in the following ways:

- ✓ Recognize what emotions are and their influence on your life Recognize how emotions develop and how you may use them for personal progress.
- ✓ Recognize the negative emotions that dominate your life and develop the skills necessary to overcome them.

✓ Change your narrative in order to regain control of your life and envision a more appealing future.

✓ Rewire your brain to be more receptive to good feelings. Confront unpleasant emotions and train your brain to generate more positive ones.

✓ Acquire all of the necessary tools to begin detecting and regulating your emotions.

A more extensive explanation of what you'll study in this book is as follows:

In **Part I**, we'll define emotions. You'll discover why your brain is programmed to concentrate on negative and how to overcome this tendency. Additionally, you'll learn how your beliefs affect your emotions. Finally, you'll have an understanding of how negative emotions function and why they're so perplexing.

In **Part II**, we'll discuss the factors that have a direct effect on your emotions. You'll get a better understanding of the roles that your body, thoughts, words, and sleep play in your life and how you may utilize them to alter your emotions.

In **Part III**, you'll discover how emotions develop and how to train your mind to feel more pleasant feelings.

Finally, in **Part IV**, we'll examine how to harness the power of your emotions for personal development. You'll discover why and how you feel emotions such as fear or despair.

Let's begin.

PART I

The Nature of Emotions

Have you ever wondered what emotions are or how they function?

We'll explain how your survival mechanism affects your emotions in this part. Then, we'll define the 'ego' and discuss how it affects your emotions. Finally, we'll dissect the mechanics of emotion and examine why dealing with unpleasant emotions may be so difficult.

Emotions and Your Survival Mechanism

Why do individuals have a tendency towards negativity?

Your brain is intended for survival, which is why you are reading this book right now. Consider if the chance of your birth was exceedingly remote. For this miracle to occur, all previous generations had to live long enough to reproduce. They must have faced death hundreds, if not thousands of times in their struggle for survival and breeding.

Fortunately, unlike your forefathers and mothers, you are (probably) not confronted with mortality on a daily basis. Indeed, life has never been safer in many areas of the globe. Despite this, your survival mechanism has remained relatively unchanged. Your brain continues to monitor your surroundings for possible hazards.

In several respects, some areas of your brain have become redundant. While you may not be seconds away from being devoured by a predator, your brain nonetheless assigns negative occurrences much more weight than happy ones.

Fear of rejection is one manifestation of a proclivity towards negativity. In the past, being rejected by your tribe drastically decreased your chances of survival. As a result, you developed an innate need to hunt for signs of rejection, which got programmed into your brain.

Nowadays, rejection typically has little or no effect on one's long-term survival. You may be universally despised and yet have a job.

Despite the fact that you have a roof over your head and enough of food on the table, your brain is still wired to see rejection as a danger to your life.

This hardwiring is one of the reasons why rejection can be so hurtful. While you are aware that the majority of rejections are insignificant, you nonetheless experience emotional distress. If you pay attention to your thoughts, you may even construct a whole drama around them. You may think you are unworthy of love and obsess for days or weeks on a rejection. Worse, as a consequence of this rejection, you may develop depression.

Frequently, a single critique outweighs hundreds of good ones. That is why an author who has fifty 5-star ratings is likely to feel depressed upon receiving a single 1-star review. While the author is aware that the one-star review does not constitute a danger to her existence, her authorial brain is not. It is possible that the bad critique is seen as a danger to her ego, eliciting an emotional response.

Fear of rejection may sometimes cause you to exaggerate occurrences. If your supervisor criticizes you at work, your brain may interpret the criticism as a threat, prompting the thought, "What if my boss fires me?" What if I am unable to get employment soon enough and my wife abandons me? How about my children? What if I'm never able to see them again?"

While you are lucky to have such an effective survival mechanism, it is your obligation to distinguish between genuine and imagined dangers. If you do not, you will face unneeded pain and concern, which will have a detrimental effect on your life's quality. To overcome this negative bias, you must rewire your thinking. One of the greatest abilities of a human being is their capacity to utilize their ideas to create their world and interpret situations in more powerful ways. This book will demonstrate how to do this.

Why isn't it your brain's responsibility to make you happy?

The basic function of your brain is not to make you happy, but to secure your life. Thus, if you want to be happy, you must actively regulate your emotions rather than relying on your natural state of happiness. We'll explore what happiness is and how it works in the next part.

Dopamine is a neurotransmitter that is involved in a variety of processes, including rewarding specific actions. When dopamine is released into certain sections of the brain referred to as the pleasure centers, you experience a strong sensation of well-being comparable to a high. This sensation of well-being occurs when you exercise, gamble, have sex, or consume delicious cuisine.

One of dopamine's functions is to guarantee that you seek food in order to avoid starving and that you seek a partner in order to reproduce. Without dopamine, our species would very certainly have perished long ago. That is a fairly fantastic thing, isn't it?

To be honest, yes and no. This incentive mechanism is often outmoded in today's environment. While dopamine was formerly intimately related to human survival, it may today be artificially increased. Social media is an excellent illustration of this effect, since it leverages psychology to squander as much time as possible from your life. Have you noticed how many alerts crop up on a daily basis? They're utilized to stimulate the release of dopamine, which helps you maintain contact, and the longer you maintain contact, the more money the services earn. Pornographic viewing and gambling both result in the release of dopamine, which may make both behaviors extremely addictive.

Fortunately, we are not required to respond whenever our brain produces dopamine. For instance, we are not required to constantly monitor our Facebook newsfeeds. Simply because it provides us with a delightful dose of dopamine.

Today's culture promotes a notion of happiness that has the potential to make us unhappy. We developed an addiction to dopamine mostly as a result of marketers discovering effective methods to manipulate our brains. We get repeated dopamine doses throughout the day, which we like. However, is this synonymous with happiness?

Worse still, dopamine has the potential to develop true addictions, which may have a negative impact on our health. Tulane University research found that when individuals were allowed to self-stimulate their pleasure centers, they did so an average of forty times each minute. They prioritized pleasure center stimulation above food, sometimes refusing to eat when hungry!

Lee Seung Seop, a Korean, is a severe example of this condition. Mr Seop died in 2005 after spending fifty-eight hours straight playing a computer game with minimal food or drink and no sleep. Following an autopsy, it was determined that the cause of death was heart failure caused by tiredness and dehydration. He was twenty-eight years old at the time.

To regain control of your emotions, it's necessary to grasp dopamine's function and how it affects your happiness. Are you a phone addict? Are you a slave to your television? Or maybe you spend an inordinate amount of time playing video games. The majority of us are dependent on something. For some, this is self-evident, while for others, it is more nuanced. For instance, you may be dependent on your ability to think. To regain control of your emotions, you must identify and confront your addictions, which may rob you of your happiness.

Myth of the 'one day I shall'

Do you think that you will one day realize your goal and be really happy? This is quite improbable. You may attain your objective (and

I hope you do), but you will not live 'happily ever after.' This way of thinking is another deception perpetrated by your mind.

Your mind adapts fast to new settings, which is most likely a product of evolution and our constant need to adapt in order to live and reproduce.

This acclimation is also likely why the new automobile or home you want will bring you happiness only temporarily. After the first thrill wears off, you'll desire the next interesting thing. This is referred to as 'hedonic adaptation.'

The mechanism through which hedonic adaptation occurs

Permit me to present an intriguing research that will almost certainly alter your perception of happiness. This 1978 research on lottery winners and paraplegics was quite eye-opening for me. The study examined the effect of winning the lottery or being paraplegic on happiness:

The research discovered that both groups were exactly as pleased a year afterwards as they were before to the incident. Yes, I am equally delighted (or unhappy). More information on it may be found by viewing Dan Gilbert's TED Talk, The Surprising Science of Happiness, here.

Perhaps you think that after you've made it,' you'll be happy. However, as the preceding research on happiness demonstrates, this is simply not true. Whatever occurs to you, your mind will automatically return to your predefined degree of happiness after you've acclimated to the new situation.

Is this to say that you cannot be happy than you are now? No. This suggests that, over time, external events have a negligible effect on your degree of satisfaction.

Indeed, according to Sonja Lyubomirsky, author of The How of Happiness, genetics account for 50% of our happiness, internal variables account for 40%, and external influences account for 10%. These external elements include our status as single or married, wealthy or impoverished, and similar societal influences.

External influences generally have a much less impact than you imagined. The main line is that your attitude toward life, not what happens to you, determines your happiness.

You now understand how your survival mechanism has a detrimental effect on your emotions and hinders you from feeling greater pleasure and happiness in life. The next section will discuss the ego.

Understanding the Ego

Not just your survival mechanism has an effect on your emotions. Your ego also has a huge influence on how you feel. Thus, in order to regain control of your emotions, it is critical that you grasp what an ego is and how it functions.

Now, let us define ego. We often refer to someone as having a "large ego," referring to the ego as something akin to pride. While pride is unquestionably an expression of ego, it is simply one aspect of it. You may seem to be self-effacing and modest while yet being ruled by your ego.

What, then, is the ego?

The ego is a term that refers to the self-identity you've developed throughout the course of your life. How did this persona come to be? Simply said, the ego is a mental construct that was generated by your ideas and, as a mind-made identity, lacks any actual existence.

The events that occur to you are meaningless in and of themselves. They have significance only as a result of your perception of those occurrences. Additionally, you accept aspects of yourself because others have instructed you to. Additionally, you identify similarly with your name, your age, your religion, your political beliefs, and your profession.

This connection has ramifications. As we will see later in this book, attachment results in the formation of beliefs, which then result in the experiencing of certain emotions. For example, you may get offended if someone criticizes your religious or political convictions.

Please take note that throughout this book, we will refer to the ego as your 'story' or 'identity,' using these terms interchangeably.

Are you aware of your own ego?

Your comprehension of how your ego functions is contingent upon your degree of self-awareness. Individuals at the lowest level of awareness are unaware of the ego's existence and are hence enslaved by it.

On the other hand, persons who are very self-conscious may see through their ego. They grasp how belief works and how an unhealthy fixation on a certain set of beliefs may result in suffering in their lives. In effect, these folks gain control of their minds and achieve self-acceptance.

Bear in mind that the ego is neither good nor evil; it is just a symptom of a lack of self-awareness. It dissipates as you gain consciousness of it, since ego and awareness cannot coexist.

Your ego's need for identity

Your ego is a self-centered creature that is exclusively concerned with its own survival. Interestingly, it acts in a manner similar to that of your brain. It has a survival mechanism and will go to any length to ensure its existence. As with your brain, it is not preoccupied with your pleasure or peace of mind. Your ego, on the other hand, is restless. It desires that you be a go-getter. It desires for you to perform, acquire, and accomplish big things in order for you to become a 'someone.'

As previously said, your ego needs an identity in order to live. It does this via associating with objects, people, or beliefs and ideas.

Now, let's examine some of the strategies your ego employs to maintain its identity:

Physical objects

The ego enjoys identifying with material possessions. It survives and flourishes in today's world. Perhaps we might argue that capitalism and the consumer culture in which we now live are the product of collective egos, which is why they have been the dominant economic paradigm for the last several decades.

Marketers are well aware of people's need to identify with objects. They understand that consumers do not only purchase a thing; they also purchase the emotions or narrative associated with the goods.

Frequently, you purchase special clothing or a particular automobile in order to convey a narrative about yourself. For example, you may like to elevate your status, seem cool, or exhibit your distinct individuality, and pick things that reflect these goals.

The ego operates by using objects to build a tale with which you can identify. This does not always imply that anything is wrong. It becomes a problem only when you develop an unhealthy attachment to worldly possessions, thinking they can complete you —which they cannot.

Your physical structure

The majority of individuals acquire their self-worth from their looks. Your ego loves the way you appear because it is the most easily identifiable and quantifiable aspect of you. When you have a strong connection to your physical appearance, you are more likely to identify with bodily and emotional discomfort. Whether you believe it or not, you can watch your body without 'identification' with it.

Friends/acquaintances

Additionally, the ego obtains its sense of self-identity from your interactions with others. The ego is primarily concerned with obtaining something from others. In other words, the ego lives on its ability to develop its identity via the manipulation of others.

If you're honest with yourself, you'll see that the majority of your actions are motivated by a need for acceptance from others. You want that your parents are proud of you, that your employer respects you, and that your wife loves you.

Now, let us examine the ego in further depth in the following situations:

Relations between parents and children

Certain parents' egos contribute to their children developing a strong feeling of connection and identity. This attachment is founded on the erroneous assumption that their children are 'possessions.' As a consequence, parents attempt to exert influence over their children's lives and 'exploit' them to live the life they desired as children—a process known as living vicariously via your children. This occurs often. When you next attend a junior soccer (or baseball) game, pay attention to how certain parents behave on the touchline. Consider identifying the parents who are living vicariously via their children— they are the ones who are yelling the loudest, and not only in support. This is often unintentional.

Couples

The sensation of needing someone is also very much an ego game. Once you accept that you do not need anybody, you may begin to appreciate other people's company. You can see people for who they really are rather than attempting to coerce them.

Your convictions

Additionally, your ego employs beliefs to fortify its identity. In extreme circumstances, individuals grow so devoted to their ideals that they are willing to die to safeguard them. Worse worse, they are prepared to murder anyone who oppose them. Religion is an excellent example of the problems associated with an unhealthy commitment to one's ideas. The ego will exploit any belief to bolster its identity, whether religious, political, or philosophical in nature.

Additional identifiers

Now, let's have a look at a (non-exhaustive) list of the broad sources of your ego's identity:

- ✓ Your physical structure
- ✓ Your given name
- ✓ Your sexual orientation
- ✓ Your country of origin
- ✓ Your cultural heritage
- ✓ Your relatives/friends
- ✓ Your convictions (political beliefs, religious, etc.)
- ✓ Your personal narrative (your interpretation of the past, your expectations regarding the future)
- ✓ Your difficulties (illnesses, financial situation, victim mindset, etc.)
- ✓ Your chronological age
- ✓ Your occupation
- ✓ Your social standing
- ✓ Your function (as employee, homemaker, parental status, employment status, etc.)
- ✓ Substantial things (your house, car, clothes, phone, etc.)
- ✓ Your aspirations

The primary qualities of the ego

The following are some of the ego's primary characteristics:

✓ Because the ego tends to link 'having' with 'being,' it is attracted to items.

✓ The ego survives on the basis of comparison. Your ego is always comparing itself to other egos.

✓ The ego is always dissatisfied. Your ego is always hungry for more. Increased renown, material possessions, and recognition, and so on.

✓ The ego's feeling of self-worth is often contingent on your perceived value in the eyes of others. To feel important, your ego needs the approval of others.

The ego's insatiable need to feel superior

Your ego desires a sense of superiority over other egos. It wants to distinguish itself and must thus establish false divisions. The following are some of the tactics it employs:

Increasing its worth via the use of people. If you have intelligent/famous pals, your ego will gravitate toward them in order to bolster its identity.

This is why some individuals like bragging about their friends' intelligence, wealth, or celebrity.

Gossip. Individuals chatter in order to feel different and superior in some manner. This is why some individuals like putting others down and talking behind their backs; it makes them feel superior, as does everyone else in their gossiping circle.

Showing signs of an inferiority complex. This conceals a desire to feel superior to others. Yes, even in this instance, individuals want a sense of superiority.

Suffering with a superiority complex, this conceals the worry of not being adequate.

Seeking notoriety. This creates a sense of superiority, which is why many individuals want to be renowned.

Being correct. The ego is obsessed with being accurate. It's a wonderful method for it to establish itself. Have you noticed that everyone believes they are doing the right thing, from Adolf Hitler to Nelson Mandela?

Complaints. The majority of individuals believe they are accurate. However, can everyone be correct? By definition, when individuals complain, they feel they are right and others are wrong. It also works with things.

Have you ever collided with a table and expressed your displeasure or even insulted it? I have, and wasn't it a mistake for the damned table to be in my way?

Attracting attention. The ego thrives on being seen. It thrives on acknowledgment, praise, and adoration. To get attention, individuals may also commit crimes, dress eccentrically, or cover their body with tattoos.

The influence of your ego on your emotions

Understanding how your ego functions may assist you in exercising more control over your emotions. To begin, you must recognize that your present tale is the product of a strong affinity with people, things, or ideas. This strong identification is at the basis of a great deal of the unpleasant feelings you encounter in life. Consider the following:

When life does not develop as planned, or when someone questions one of your beliefs, you get defensive.

In summary, the majority of your emotions are determined by your personal narrative and your worldview. You will be able to feel more pleasant emotions when you replace your present tale with a more empowered one—while simultaneously letting go of your excessive connection to things, people, or ideas. Later in this book, we'll examine how you might alter your interpretation of events.

Factors involved in emotion

Emotions may be perplexing. We'll explore how they operate in detail in this section. By understanding the process behind emotions, you may more effectively handle them when they emerge.

To begin, it is necessary to recognize that feelings are transitory. You may feel pleased one minute and depressed the next. While you have some influence over your emotions, you must equally acknowledge their irrationality. You set yourself up for failure if you expect to be happy all of the time. You then risk blaming yourself or, worse, beating yourself up when you 'fail' to be happy.

To begin regaining control of your emotions, you must first acknowledge their transitory nature. You must learn to let them go without feeling compelled to connect with them deeply. Allow yourself to be sad without interjecting comments such as "I shouldn't be sad" or "What's wrong with me?" Rather than that, you must allow reality to just be.

No matter how psychologically strong you are, you will suffer sorrow, loss, or despair at some point in your life—hopefully not simultaneously or on a consistent basis. You may experience moments of disappointment, betrayal, insecurity, resentment, or embarrassment. You'll begin to question yourself and your capacity to be the person you want. However, this is OK since emotions arrive and, more importantly, they disappear.

Your negative feelings are neither harmful nor ineffective.

You may blame yourself for bad feelings or believe that you are psychologically weak. You may even feel there is something fundamentally wrong with you. Regardless of what your inner monologue says, your feelings are not negative. Simply said, emotions are feelings. Not much more.

As example, being unhappy does not diminish your worth as a person in comparison to three weeks earlier when you were joyful. Being depressed at the moment does not imply you will never be able to laugh again.

Bear in mind that it is your interpretation of emotions, as well as your blame game, that causes suffering, not the feelings themselves.

Negative emotions, on the other hand, may be beneficial. Occasionally, you must hit rock bottom in order to reach the summit. Even the most tenacious individuals on the planet may succumb to depression. Elon Musk never anticipated having a mental breakdown, but he did and he recovered. Abraham Lincoln was despondent for months after the loss of his fiancée. This sad occurrence had no effect on his election to the presidency of the United States. Oftentimes, negative feelings have a purpose. They might be a wake-up call. They could assist you in discovering something wonderful about yourself. Of course, when you're under their spell, it's impossible to see the good side, but in retrospect, you may see that emotions—even negative ones—played a part in your eventual success.

Your emotions are not there to complicate your life, but to communicate with you. You would not be able to develop without them.

Consider the bad feelings you are experiencing as the emotional counterpart of physical pain. While you may despise being in pain, the likelihood is that you would be dead by now if not for pain. Physical discomfort is a strong indicator that something is wrong, prompting you to take action. It might be to visit your physician, who may recommend surgery, dietary changes, or more activity. Without physical discomfort, none of them would be possible.

Things and your position would deteriorate, maybe resulting in an early death.

Emotions operate similarly. They urge you to take action in light of your existing circumstances. Perhaps you need to let go of certain relationships, resign your career, or eliminate a disempowering tale that is causing you pain.

Emotions' transitory nature

This too must pass, regardless of how miserable you are, how much pain you are suffering, or how awful you feel at any particular moment.

Consider some of the bad feelings you've already encountered. Consider the darkest periods of your life. During these most trying times, you were undoubtedly so consumed by your emotions that you felt you would never be able to escape them. You couldn't conceive of ever feeling joyful again. However, even these instances came to an end. Eventually, the veils cleared, revealing the true you.

Emotions come and go. Your despair will lift, your grief will dissipate, and your rage will subside.

Bear in mind that if you frequently feel the same emotions, it is likely that you have disempowering ideas and need to make a change in your life. This will be discussed later.

If you suffer from severe, persistent depression, it may be prudent to seek treatment from a professional.

Emotional deception

Have you ever felt as though you'd never again be happy? Have you ever been so enamored with your feelings that you believed they would never leave?

Not to worry; this is a usual reaction.

Negative emotions work as a filter on your experiences, distorting their quality. Every encounter is filtered via this filter during a bad episode.

While the world outside may stay same, you will see it in an entirely different light depending on your state of mind.

For example, when you're sad, you lose interest in the food you consume, the movies you watch, and the activities you participate in. You notice only the worst aspects of situations, feeling imprisoned and helpless. On the other hand, when one is in a good mood, everything looks to be better. Food tastes amazing, you like all of your activities, and you're naturally more sociable.

You may now think that armed with the information contained in this book, you will never experience depression again. Wrong! You will continue to experience sorrow, frustration, despair, or resentment, but each time, you will hopefully grow in wisdom, knowing that this, too, will pass.

I have to confess that my emotions may easily trick me. While I am aware that I am not my emotions, I continue to give them too much credence and fail to see they are just passing through. More significantly, I am oblivious to the fact that they are not me. Emotions come and go, but I am always present. After the emotional storm subsides, I often feel foolish for taking my sentiments so seriously. Do you agree?

External stimuli, however, are often not the immediate source of a quick shift in your mental state. You may be in the same circumstances, with the same work, the same bank account balance, and the same issues as before, yet experience dramatically different emotional states. Indeed, if you examine your own history, this is often the case. You experience minor depression for a few hours or days before reverting to your 'normal' emotional state. Throughout this time of mental distress, your surroundings remain unchanged. Only your internal discourse remains constant.

I advise you to make a deliberate effort to observe when such situations occur and to develop an ability to see through your emotions' deception. You may want to take it a step further and keep a notebook of these incidents. This will give you a greater knowledge of how emotions function and, as a consequence; will enable you to regulate them more effectively.

Emotions' destructive power

Negative emotions have the power to cast a spell. While you are under their influence, it seems hard to escape. While you may be aware that repeating the same ideas is futile, you can't help but go with the flow. With a strong pull, you continue to connect with your ideas, making you feel worse and worse. When this occurs, no sensible argument seems to be effective.

The more these emotions resonate with your own narrative, the more powerful the attraction. For instance, if you feel you are not good enough, you may experience unpleasant emotions such as guilt or shame whenever you evaluate your actions to be 'insufficient.' Because you've encountered these feelings several times before, they've developed into an instinctive reaction.

Refer to the section "Identification" for further information on how identification with emotions works.

Emotions' filtering ability

Your emotional state may have a profound effect on your perspective on life, causing you to act and behave differently.

When you are in a good mood, you have more energy accessible to you. This energy bestows upon you the following:

Increased assurance in whatever you do

Your emotional state may have a profound effect on your view on life, influencing how you act and behave.

When you are in a negative frame of mind, you have less energy accessible to you, which results in the following:

✓   A lack of confidence that pervades your actions

- ✓ A lack of drive that limits the range of activities you are ready to conduct A unwillingness to confront new problems and go beyond your comfort zone
- ✓ A diminished capacity for perseverance in the face of failures, and a proclivity for negative thinking within the same emotional range.

Allow me to illustrate this with a true story from my own life. Both instances occurred under the same external circumstances. The only difference was that I was in a different emotional condition at the time.

Case 1 - I'm delighted with my internet business:

- ✓ Increased confidence in whatever I do: I believe my ideas are sound. I'm looking forward to working on my books and writing articles. I am open to sharing and promoting my work.
- ✓ A willingness to examine other courses of action: I am open to fresh ideas and the possibility of working on a new project. I can think of ways to collaborate with other authors and start building a new coaching program to offer my audience.
- ✓ The capacity to push myself beyond my comfort zone: I'm finding it simpler to push myself beyond my comfort zone. I may contact strangers or manage 'Facebook Lives,' for example.
- ✓ More emotional space for perseverance: I stay with my work even when I'm feeling unmotivated.
- ✓ Improved thoughts and more creativity: I am receptive to fresh ideas. I may have fresh ideas for books, articles, or other creative endeavors.

✓   Access to more happy emotions is simple: I draw additional pleasant feelings. Simultaneously, by refusing to connect with negative ideas, my mind rejects them more effectively.

Case 2 - Suffering from minor depression as a consequence of my lack of results:

Lack of confidence: I begin to mistrust myself and the tasks on which I am now working. Suddenly, whatever I do becomes ineffective or 'insufficient.' I have thoughts such as "What's the point?" "I'm not going to make it," and "I'm dumb." Self-promotion becomes a huge obstacle.

A lack of motivation: I'm not in the mood to accomplish anything. I am bombarded by negative ideas and unable to avoid them. I experience the same unpleasant ideas again, as if they were a broken record. They seem to be so genuine that they poison all of my encounters.

Difficulty accepting new challenges: I lack the energy necessary to leave my comfort zone and embark on new endeavors.

A diminished capacity for perseverance: I have difficulties completing projects and delay on chores that should be completed.

A proclivity for attracting bad ideas: I am attracting an increasing number of unpleasant thoughts. Although these ideas may have crossed my head before, they now cling to me. By associating with these beliefs, I amplify unpleasant feelings.

Both incidents occurred within a few days of one another. The exterior world remained same, but my mental state shifted dramatically, causing me to conduct different behaviors.

Emotions' magnetic force

Your emotions have a magnetic effect. They attract ideas that are traveling on the same 'wave.' That is why, when you are in a bad condition, you are prone to attract further negative ideas, and by hanging on to them, you exacerbate the issue.

Now, let us examine what you can do to disassociate yourself from that magnetic force.

Dismantling the magnetic attraction of emotions

Assume you're having a rough day at work and are in a foul mood. Your bad mood attracts other negative ideas. Suddenly, you get obsessed with the idea that you're still unmarried at thirty and begin to beat yourself up over it. Then you begin to blame yourself for your obesity. Additionally, you recall that you have to go to work the next Saturday, which serves as a reminder of how much your job stinks.

Consider how much simpler it is to attract bad ideas when you are depressed. To avoid this, one must break the tendency of grouping unpleasant ideas together.

Real-world illustration:

I have knee issues, which hinder me from participating in a variety of activities. Because I've always been a sports fan, these injuries have caused me mental distress. Fortunately, I seldom have knee discomfort, but when I do, it might elicit unpleasant feelings. As I observed my mental process one day, I recognized that having pain in my knees had a bad effect on my mood, creating further unpleasant feelings in a negative feedback loop. The

Pain drew my attention to everything that was wrong, from my career to my personal life. As a consequence, I'd be overcome with bad feelings for hours, if not days.

The point I'm making is that regardless of how wonderful your life is, if you spend the most of your time dwelling on your difficulties, you will get depression. Thus, in order to mitigate bad emotions, you must have the ability to compartmentalize your concerns. Allow your imagination to overdramatize events by grouping unconnected events together. It will simply serve to exacerbate your distress. Rather than that, keep in mind that bad feelings exist just in your head. Taken individually, the majority of your problems aren't that significant, and there is no rule requiring you to resolve them all at once.

Begin by observing your feelings. Keep a journal of your unpleasant feelings. Consider what causes them. The more you practice this, the more definite patterns will emerge. For instance, if you've been feeling down for a few days, ask yourself the following questions:

- ✓ What set off my emotions?
- ✓ What kept them going for two days? What was the narrative I was telling myself?
- ✓ How and why did I emerge from my funk? How can I use what I've learned from this episode?

Responding to these questions will be quite beneficial and will greatly assist you in dealing with similar difficulties in the future.

Previously, we saw how you drew ideas that corresponded to your emotional condition. Likewise, the converse is true. You cannot attract ideas that are out of step with your current state of mind. Even if you attempted to think happy things, your mind would be impregnated with negativity. This is why, although happy ideas may sometimes reach your mind during times of melancholy, you will be unable to correlate them with them and hence will be unable to alter your emotional state.

Have you ever been urged to brighten up at a time of grief or to show thankfulness during a time of depression? Was it beneficial? It most likely did not. This is because the emotional state in which you were was preventing you from experiencing these feelings.

Ester and Jerry Hicks provide a concept in their book, Ask and it is given that explains how emotional ranges are related and how we may go from negative to positive emotions. For example, under this approach, despair or hopelessness is ranked lowest, followed by fury. That instance, when you are sad, symptoms of rage imply that you are progressing up the emotional ladder. This is reasonable. When one is furious, one has more energy than when one is down, correct?

I just had sentiments of fury after a period of depression. For whatever reason, I became weary of the tales and justifications that ran through my head, and I utilized my anger to propel me forward toward doing the duties I had been avoiding. As a consequence, I gained momentum and ascended the emotional ladder.

When you are experiencing negative emotions, keep an eye out for those that provide you with more energy. So-called negative emotions, such as rage, may actually assist you in overcoming more disempowering feelings, such as despair. Only you are aware of your emotions. As a result, if rage makes you feel better, embrace it.

Emotional distress and mental anguish

Did you realize that you cause yourself a great deal of unneeded suffering in your life? Each time you get fixated on a notion or a feeling, you suffer. A good illustration of this is how you respond to bodily discomfort. When you experience pain, your first response is to interpret it. This results in the generation of negative ideas. Mental suffering is caused by your connection with these ideas. The following are some of the possibilities that may occur to you in these situations:

What if this discomfort never subsides?

What if I am unable to do X, Y, or Z due to pain? What if the situation deteriorates?

What if I need surgery?

What if I am unable to work? I'm working on a critical project that I need to complete on time.

Today is going to be difficult with this ache, and I don't have any money. How am I going to pay my medical fees if things deteriorate further?

This mental discussion causes suffering but contributes nothing to resolving the issue. You can continue to operate normally and take appropriate measures even if you are preoccupied with any of the aforementioned concerns. The issue is not with negative emotions; it is with the mental suffering that these feelings cause.

Procrastination is another type of mental anguish. Have you ever put off beginning a job for days or weeks just to discover how trivial it was once completed? Yes, I have. Which portion of the activity was the most draining, the task itself or the time spent thinking about it?

Or maybe you didn't get enough sleep and are constantly reminding yourself that today is going to be a difficult day. You're already fatigued as you consider all the things that need to be completed.

Psychologists have shown that mental suffering takes the majority of your energy. After all, sitting at a desk all day should not be that exhausting, but many of us report feeling fatigued at the end of the day.

Individuals inflict an enormous amount of suffering on themselves. As you continue to read this book, you will come to appreciate the absurdity of this pastime. You'll

Take note of those around you who are fixated on a past they cannot change. You'll witness your relatives and friends fretting about an uncertain future. You'll see folks repeating the same ideas, going in circles in an attempt to solve an issue that exists only in their heads. For thousands of years, mystics have taught us that our issues are psychological in nature. They have continually urged us to examine ourselves. Yet how many people are listening today?

Too many of us have developed an addiction to our issues. Rather of letting go, we grumble, play the victim, point the finger at others, or pontificate about our problems without taking any action to resolve them. To alleviate this mental anguish, we must resist the temptation to interpret our feelings negatively and dis-empoweringly.

If we take it a step further and look at reality objectively, we may conclude that issues do not exist. This is why:

What you do not concentrate on does not exist. A issue occurs only when you pay attention to it. From your mind's viewpoint, anything you are not thinking about does not exist. Consider the following hypothetical situation. Consider the possibility that you've lost your legs. Accepting that reality instantly and refusing to think about it creates no difficulty and consequently no mental suffering. You would just be living in reality (which is seldom the case).

A issue persists only for a limited period of time. A issue may exist only in the past or future. And, more importantly, where do the past and future exists? Within your head. To recognize an issue, you must use your ideas, which exist in time, not in the current instant.

An issue must be identified as such in order for it to exist. A issue occurs only when a circumstance is seen as a problem. Otherwise, there are no complications.

While this notion may seem difficult at first, it is a basic theory. In the next part, we'll examine the several factors that affect your emotions.

PART II

What influences your emotions?

The complexity of emotions and how you feel is influenced by a wide range of circumstances. We'll discuss some of the factors that influence your emotions in this section. As a positive side effect, you have a degree of influence on them.

Most of your emotions are self-created if we eliminate spontaneous emotional responses originating from your survival system. They're the product of how you understand ideas or situations, in other words. However, these aren't the only factors that influence your mental well-being; there are many more factors. Whether it's the quality of your emotions or the quality of your life, your body, voice, diet, and sleep all play a part.

Observe how each of these factors affects you.

Sleep's Effect on Your Mood

Sleep quality and quantity have an effect on your emotional state. You've undoubtedly personally encountered the negative consequences of sleep deprivation. Perhaps you experienced grumpiness, inability to focus, listlessness, or difficulties coping with unpleasant emotions.

Sleep deprivation may have a variety of distinct effects on mood.

According to a poll of adults with anxiety or depression, the majority of respondents reported sleeping fewer than six hours each night.

Additionally, sleep deprivation raises the chance of death. According to a 2016 study undertaken by experts at the non-profit organization RAND Europe, those who sleep fewer than six hours each night have a thirteen percent greater risk of death compared to those who sleep between seven and nine hours. The same study discovered that sleep deprivation costs the US economy an estimated $411 billion each year.

Notably, sleep deprivation seems to impair an individual's capacity for happy experiences. While those who get adequate sleep do benefit from such experiences, those who are sleep deprived do not.

How to boost your sleep quality

There are several methods for enhancing the quality of your sleep. Let us examine a few of them:

Ascertain that your bedroom is completely dark. Numerous studies have shown that the darker the bedroom, the better we sleep. What can you do to make your room darker if it isn't pitch-black? Perhaps you might get a sleep mask or drapes that filter out more light.

Eliminate the use of technological gadgets. This is true for smartphones, tablets, and TVs, among other devices. According to SleepFoundation.org, "studies have shown that even our tiniest electronic gadgets generate enough light to confuse the brain and increase awake." As

As adults, we are influenced by these forces, and our children are as well as "very vulnerable ". A 2014 research published in PNAS found that individuals who read with a melatonin supplement had a 50% reduction in melatonin, a hormone that helps regulate sleep patterns.

Rather of books, technological gadgets are preferred. These subjects fell asleep around 10 minutes later and missed ten minutes of deep sleep (also known as REM). Additionally, participants reported feeling less energized in the morning. Whether your gadget has a night mode, it may still have a detrimental effect on your sleep, but try the night mode to see if it affects your sleep habits. If you are compelled to utilize technological gadgets after dark,

Consider using blue-blocking glasses to counteract the blue light they produce. It is recommended that you put on the glasses a few hours before going to bed.

Your thoughts should be relaxed. If you're anything like me, you may find yourself thinking about a variety of things when it's time to sleep. I'm often giddy with excitement about new ideas or projects. As a consequence, I often feel as if there are so many tasks I might have accomplished throughout the day, which makes sleeping difficult. Apart from shutting off electronic gadgets before to going to bed, I've discovered that listening to relaxing music is quite beneficial. Reading a physical book may also help me unwind (as long as I avoid being too absorbed in the story, which has been known to happen.)

Avoid excessive water consumption within two hours of going to bed. This one is self-evident, but it bears noting. If you wake up in the middle of the night to use the restroom, this will disrupt your sleep pattern. Naturally, this will make you more exhausted the following day.

Establish a nightly routine. This alone will aid in your sleep. It is recommended that you attempt to go to bed at the same hour every night, including weekends. If you like going out on weekends and staying up late, this will be difficult, but I advise you to give it a go and see how it works. Additionally, a nighttime routine will assist you in adhering to your morning habit. If you have a morning and a bedtime routine, it will be simpler to get up at the same time every day without feeling weary. If you do go out and stay up late on weekends, one thing you can do is get up as early as you do on weekdays and take as many naps as required during the day.

If you're having trouble sleeping, consider implementing some of the suggestions above. My greatest suggestion is to keep experimenting with various tactics until you discover what works best for you.

Controlling Your Emotions with Your Body

The body's language and posture

By altering your body language and posture, you may vary your mood. When you are confident or joyful, your body expands and you become larger. Have you ever observed how men's backs straighten, their chests expand, and their stomachs clench when they view a beautiful woman? That is an unconscious action intended to convey confidence and authority (the same way gorillas pound their chests).

Amy Cuddy, a social psychologist at Harvard Business School, demonstrated in one of her tests that individuals who assumed a high-power position for two minutes exhibited qualities associated with confident and strong people. More precisely, she became aware of the following hormonal changes.

After two minutes in a high-power pose:

- Testosterone levels rose by 25%,
- Cortisol levels reduced by 10%
- Risk tolerance improved, with 86% of individuals opting to play a chance game

After two minutes in a low-power pose:

- Testosterone levels reduced by 10%,
- Cortisol levels rose by 15%.

- Risk tolerance reduced, with just 60% of individuals opting to play a chance game.

As you can see, adjusting your body position or facial expression may truly alter how you feel. This is referred to as "fake it till you make it." For instance, you may fake a grin to make yourself feel better. On the other hand, by altering your body position, you might have a detrimental effect on your mood and even precipitate despair.

The advantages of exercise

According to Michael Otto, a psychology professor at Boston University, "failing to exercise while you are feeling ill is equivalent to consciously refusing to take aspirin when your head aches."

When it came time for 'David Kent' to resurrect David K. Reynolds, what do you believe he needed to do? He required a shift in his body posture. Simple to say but difficult to do when you are severely depressed. Of course, he was the one who understood this better than everyone else. Despite his reluctance, he had to coerce himself into physical activity. As he increased his physical activity and became more occupied, he felt better and better until he healed completely.

David Kent's experience demonstrates how regular exercise improves not just physical health but also emotions. Exercise has been proven in studies to be equally helpful as antidepressants in treating mild to severe depression. In one research, clinical psychologist James Blumenthal of Duke University randomly assigned sedentary people with serious depressive disorders to one of four groups: supervised exercise, home-based exercise, antidepressant treatment, or a placebo tablet. Blumenthal discovered that participants in the exercise and antidepressant group had the greatest rates of remission after four months. He concluded by stating that exercise has a similar impact to antidepressants.

Blumenthal noticed that when he followed up with the same patients a year later, those who continued to exercise consistently had lower depression levels than those who exercised intermittently. Exercise seems to be beneficial not just for treating depression, but also for preventing recurrence. Therefore, when it comes to managing your emotions, include exercise in your toolkit.

Fortunately, you do not need to run 10 miles daily to benefit from exercise. Walking for thirty minutes five days a week may be really beneficial. Two and a half hours of moderate exercise every week, according to study published in PLoS Medicine, might add three and a quarter years to your life. Another study of 5,000 persons in Denmark found that those who engaged in regular physical activity lived five to seven years longer than their sedentary peers.

Exercise has both immediate and long-term advantages on your mood. According to psychology professor Michael Otto, you often experience a mood-enhancing impact within five minutes of engaging in moderate exercise. Additionally, as previously shown, consistent exercise improves long-term mental health and may be as beneficial as antidepressants.

- And how about you?
- Which activity are you planning to engage in to help you maintain your mental and physical health?

Controlling Your Emotions with Your Thoughts

Your ideas form who you are and shape the world you experience. That is why you should direct your thoughts toward what you want, not toward what you do not desire. As success guru Brian Tracy puts it, "the secret to success is to direct our conscious minds toward what we want, not toward what we fear."

Meditation's advantages

In Buddhism, the mind is sometimes referred to as the "monkey mind," since Buddhists think human thoughts are analogous to those of a monkey swinging incessantly among trees. They are strewn throughout and never seem to end. Meditation assists in taming the monkey and alleviating its restlessness. While meditating, you become aware of the constant stream of ideas that enter your mind. With practice, you develop the ability to disengage from ideas, so diminishing their force and influence. As a consequence, you'll have less unpleasant feelings and a greater sense of tranquility.

Did you know that your subconscious cannot tell the difference between genuine and 'false' experiences? This implies that you may deceive your mind via vision by recreating desirable sensations. The more details you envision, the more realistic the event will seem to your brain.

By inducing good emotions such as thankfulness, enthusiasm, or joy via visualization, you may teach your mind to experience more positive emotions, as discussed in further detail in the section "Conditioning your mind."

Impacting Your Emotions through Your Words

Your words have a greater influence on your ideas and actions than you are aware of. Because your ideas, words, and actions are all interrelated, they have an effect on one another. When you lack confidence, for example, you may employ phrases such as "I'll try," "I hope," or "I want." On the other hand, employing precise terms might erode your confidence. This also implies that specific statements, such as "I will," might help enhance your confidence. For example, declaring "I will change careers" or "I will finish this project by the end of this month" will instill greater confidence in you than declaring "I hope I can change careers" or "I'll attempt to complete this project by the end of this month."

To boost your confidence, substitute self-doubting phrases with confident ones, as seen below.

Avoid the following terms:

- Would/could/should/might Try/hope/wish
- Maybe/perhaps
- If everything is in order If everything goes according to plan

Alternatively, the following terms should be used:

- I will
- Absolutely
- Definitely
- Of course
- Sure
- Certainly
- Obviously
- Without any doubt
- No problem

The efficacy of affirmative statements

Positive affirmations are statements that you repeat to yourself repeatedly until they become real in your subconscious mind. They gradually train your mind to feel good feelings such as confidence or thankfulness. For further information on conditioning your mind, see the section on 'Conditioning your mind.'

How to Effectively Utilize Positive Affirmation

Utilize the present tense rather than the future tense ("I am," rather than "I shall").

Avoid negative expressions such as "I am not timid." Rather than that, substitute "I am confident."

Repeat the statement five times more.

Do it consistently for a month, ideally longer.

Simultaneously visualize and engage your emotions.

Several instances of strong affirmations include the following:

I like being assured.

I am unaffected by the good or terrible judgments of others. I am not subordinate to anybody, and no one is subordinate to me.

I love you.... (include your name and say it while staring into your eyes in the mirror, for example, "I love you, Thibaut"). Isn't that awkward?

Many thanks.

• For five minutes every day, practice positive affirmation. • Take note of statements that demonstrate a lack of dedication, confidence, or aggressiveness. Before you send an email, review it for terms such as "I'll attempt," "I should," and "I hope." Substitute "I will" or anything as aggressive for them. For the following three weeks, make a conscious effort to refrain from using phrases that convey a lack of confidence.

Additionally, Tony Robbins, the world-renowned life coach, has been utilizing what he refers to as "incantation" for decades before to meeting with a client or doing a lecture. He use both his body and certain language to get himself into the proper condition and achieve full assurance. While reciting your own affirmations, experiment with activating your body as well. Bear in mind that your words and actions have an effect on your emotions.

Effects of Breathing on Emotions

You can go days without food or sleep, but you cannot live without oxygen for more than a few minutes. While breathing should occur naturally, the reality is that many individuals are unaware of basic breathing techniques. As a consequence, they produce less energy than they might. These folks are more prone to fatigue than others, which has an effect on their mood and makes them more susceptible to unpleasant feelings.

Proper breathing has a variety of advantages. Breathing slowly helps alleviate anxiousness. Gurucharan Singh Khalsa and Yogi Bahjan discussed the following advantages of slow breathing in Breathwalk: Breathing Your Way to a Revitalized Body, Mind, and Spirit.

Eight breaths per minute: Stress relief and improved awareness.

Four breaths per minute: Greater awareness, improved visual acuity, and increased physical sensitivity.

One breathing cycle per minute: Improved coordination between the two hemispheres of the brain, remarkable reduction in anxiety, dread, and concern.

Rapid breathing techniques, such as the Breath of Fire, help you relieve stress, increase your alertness, and increase your vitality, among other advantages.

How Your Emotions Are Affected By Your Environment

Additionally, your environment has an effect on how you feel. By environment, I mean everything that surrounds you has the potential to influence you in some manner. It might be the people you associate with, the television series you watch, or the neighborhood in which you reside. Negative family, for example, might draw you down, while a cluttered workstation can be demotivating.

When I'm feeling unmotivated, I've observed that tidying my desk, cleaning my room, or sorting files on my computer often provides a burst of motivation.

For further information on how to manipulate your emotions via your surroundings, check the section 'Changing your Environment.'

The Effects of Music on Your Emotions

We are all aware that music has an effect on our emotions. Who hasn't worked out to Rocky's song? For instance, music has the ability to:

- Assist you in relaxing when you're exhausted
- Encourage you while you're feeling down
- Assist you in your efforts at the gym
- Assist you in expressing thanks and putting you in a happy emotional condition.

According to several researches, listening to cheerful music might help individuals improve their mood. A 2012 research found that listening to a happy music for twelve minutes, five times over a two-week period increased participants' good mood. It was interesting to see that it worked only with individuals who were instructed to make an effort to improve their mood. Other individuals did not notice an improvement in mood.

Another research published in 2014 shown that music may assist in reducing bad moods and increasing self-esteem, as mentioned below:

Specifically, the most substantial psychological effects of music treatments may be discovered in areas more directly connected to mood, most notably in the alleviation of depression and anxious symptoms, and in enhancement of emotional expression, communication and interpersonal skills, as well as self-esteem and life quality.

Valerie N. Stratton, Ph.D., and Annette H. Zalanowski of Penn State University conducted more research on music's influence on mood. They asked their kids to maintain two-week music journals. Stratton concluded as follows:

Not only did our sample of students report experiencing more good feelings after listening to music, but their existing favorable sentiments were amplified.

Interestingly, neither the kind of music nor the setting in which students listened to it had any effect on the outcome. Students' moods improved regardless of whether they were listening to rock or classical music, driving or socializing.

Utilizing music to train your mind

You may take this a step further by tailoring playlists to your emotional requirements. Creating playlists takes time, but is well worth the effort. Christopher Bergland, a world-class endurance athlete and coach, utilizes music to remain motivated and perform at his best. This is what he wrote in a Psychology Today article:

As an athlete, I built an ideal attitude for optimal performance and bolstered this alter ego and invincible state of mind with an arsenal of time-tested music. Throughout my training and races, it became clear that I could utilize music (and my imagination) to construct a parallel world that had nothing to do with reality, even in very horrific weather conditions or when I was physically suffering. While competing in ultra-endurance events, I utilized music to keep upbeat and perceive the glass as permanently half-full. Similarly, you may utilize music as a tool when exercising or in your everyday life.

Christopher also prefers listening to particular music before to doing a large interview or giving a public speech. Personally, I like listening to music that inspires gratitude.

And how about you?

How can music help you feel better?

Experiment with various styles of music.

Experiment with several genres of music to see how they might be used to elevate your mood. For instance, you may utilize music to assist you in meditating, exercising, or doing schoolwork. Bear the following considerations in mind while you do so:

Everyone is unique; do not listen to a music just because it is popular. Listen to it because it elicits the emotions you want. Each of us has unique musical interests. What important is how you feel when listening to music.

Continue experimenting: Listen to a variety of various styles of music and note how they affect your emotions.

- Are you moved?
- Motivated?
- Happy?
- Relaxed?

Begin by generating playlists for the feelings you'd want to experience.

PART III

Emotional Management: How to Improve Your Emotions

We'll look at ways to cope with unpleasant emotions and train your mind to feel more good ones in this part.

To begin, we'll examine how emotions are produced. Then we'll explore the benefits of positive thinking and how to shape your mind with it. Following that, we'll discuss why positive thinking alone is insufficient and what more you may do to manage unpleasant feelings. More precisely, you will learn:

- How to emancipate yourself from your emotions
- How to rewrite your narrative in a more powerful manner How to train your mind to think positively
- How to manipulate your behavior in order to alter your feelings, and
- How to alter your surroundings in order to alleviate unpleasant feelings.

Finally, I'll provide you with a list of short- and long-term tactics for dealing with unpleasant emotions.

Let's begin.

THE METHODS BY WHICH EMOTIONS ARE FORMED

Few individuals understand how emotions develop. While we are constantly confronted with them, we seldom — if ever — stop to consider why we are experiencing specific emotions and how they came to be.

To begin, let us distinguish two distinct sorts of unpleasant feelings. The first category includes unpleasant feelings that arise spontaneously. These are the emotions that sustain you, such as the dread our forefathers felt when they came face to face with a saber-toothed tiger.

The second kind of unpleasant emotions is those created in your mind as a result of identification with your ideas. These emotions are not always provoked by external events, but they often are. These feelings, on the other hand, tend to linger longer than the first. They operate as follows:

A random notion occurs to me. That is an idea with which you identify. This recognition elicits an emotional response. As you continue to connect with that notion, the associated feeling gets stronger and stronger until it develops into a core emotion. Consider the following examples:

You are experiencing financial difficulties, and each time your mind generates money-related ideas, you identify with them. As a consequence, your financial anxiety increases.

You had a fight with a buddy and ended the friendship. You find yourself reliving the incident in your thoughts incessantly. As a consequence, months have gone without you calling to apologize to your buddy.

You made an error at work and feel embarrassed. You keep returning to the same concept. As a consequence, your emotions of inadequacy become more intense.

Your propensity to continually identify with negative ideas is what fuels their growth. The more you concentrate on your money difficulties, the more likely similar ideas may surface in the future. The more times you repeat the fight with your buddy in your thoughts, the more vehement your sentiments of animosity will become. Similarly, by continually recalling the error you made at work, you foster emotions of humiliation and exacerbate the problem. The idea is that when you allow for the existence of thoughts, they expand and become focal focuses of attention.

This simple identification procedure enables apparently harmless ideas to seize control of your mind. This affiliation with your ideas, and more crucially, how you perceive them, contributes to your life's pain.

Now, let's examine how your emotions are generated in more depth. This will assist you in dealing with unpleasant emotions more effectively while enabling happy feelings to flourish. The following formula explains how emotions are formed:

Interpretation + identification + repetition = strong emotion

Interpretation is the process through which you give meaning to an event or a concept based on your unique experience.

Identification occurs when you get identified with a certain idea as it occurs.

Repetition is the act of thinking the same ideas again.

Strong emotion occurs when you have encountered a feeling so often that it has been ingrained in your identity. You then feel that emotion anytime a thought or event associated with it provokes it.

When combined, interpretation, identification, and repetition allow for the development of emotions. In contrast, when one of these factors is removed from the equation, these feelings begin to lose their hold on you.

To summarize, in order for an emotion to increase in intensity and length, you must first interpret an event or idea, then connect with that thought when it emerges, and ultimately, you must repeat the same thoughts repeatedly—and identify with them.

Now, let's dissect each component of the formula in further detail.

1. Interpretation

Interpretation + identification + repetition = strong emotion

Negative emotions are always the outcome of how you perceive situations. That is why two individuals may respond differently to the same incident. One may suffer irreparable harm, while the other may remain untouched.

For example, rain may be a godsend to a farmer, but a misery to someone going on a picnic. That is due to the significance they impart on the event. In short, you must add your interpretation to a certain occurrence in order for unpleasant feelings to develop. Without your agreement, the incident cannot elicit unpleasant feelings.

Therefore, why do you continue to experience bad emotions? That, I suppose, is because reality does not live up to your aspirations.

You want for reality to be one way, but it reveals itself to be very another.

You're going on a picnic and wish for nice weather, but it pours. You want a promotion at work but are unable to get one.

You're attempting to earn money with your side company, but it's failing.

Your perspective of reality contributes to your life's pain. Reality cannot ever be distressing in and of itself. This is a point worth emphasizing. In the next part, 'Changing your tale,' we'll examine in detail how you might alter your perspective.

2. Identification

Interpretation + identification + repetition = strong emotion

Now, let's concentrate on the formula's second component: identification.

For an emotion to persist throughout time, it must undergo an identification process. Emotions are impermanent unless you pay them attention. The more you concentrate on – and identify with — your emotions, the more powerful they become.

Individuals often feel compelled to identify with their emotions and are unable to escape from them. They are oblivious to one of the

The most fundamental realities in our universe are as follows: emotions come and go. You are not a product of your feelings. Your feelings will pass you by.

Therefore, whenever you find yourself stating, "I'm sad," keep in mind that you are mistaken. Nobody has ever felt sad, since emotions are not an integral part of who you are. They may look to be you, but like clouds in the sky, they will soon vanish. Consider yourself to be the sun, and the sun is always there whether you notice it or not—whether or not it is obscured by a cloud.

You are not a product of your feelings. You are not sad; you only have sensations that you may refer to as' sadness' at a certain moment in time. This is a critical point. I hope you notice the distinction.

Another method to see your emotions is via the lens of your clothing. What emotional garments are you now wearing? Are these garments of ecstasy? Depression? Sadness? Bear in mind that you will most likely be wearing different clothing tomorrow or in a week.

The length of time you wear your garments (your emotions) is determined by how much you adore them (i.e. how connected you are to your feelings). An feeling is impotent in and of itself. Your conscious or unconscious affiliation with it endows it with force. That is why a feeling that receives little attention gradually fades away. Consider the exercise below:

When you're upset, engage in any activity that requires your undivided focus. You'll notice that your fury swiftly subsides. On the other hand, if you continue to focus on your anger, it will increase until it becomes one of your primary emotional states.

3. Repetition

Interpretation + identification + repetition = strong emotion

As previously shown, how you perceive an event or a concept has an effect on how you feel. Additionally, we know that when you grow identified with your ideas or feelings, they develop into emotions. Now, if you repeat this practice often enough, you will train your mind to feel these exact emotions (positive or negative).

For instance, if you concentrate only on what your buddy (allegedly) did to you, resentment will rise. As a consequence, you may harbor resentment for months. This is a common occurrence. They squander time clinging to bad feelings that serve no purpose just because they are unable of letting goes.

On the other hand, if you disconnect from your resentment thoughts and merely watch them, they will gradually lose their force and the accompanying resentment will go away. Indeed, if you had promptly abandoned the concept of anger at its emergence, your sentiments of resentment would have vanished virtually instantaneously. In the section 'Letting go of your emotions,' we'll look at how you can do just that.

Taking action

Consider the last time you experienced an emotion such as anger, sorrow, irritation, fear, or despair. Now, jot down what occurs in each of the following situations:

- What events transpired and what ideas arose?
- How did you react to these thoughts?
- Did you repeatedly identify with these thoughts?

Improving Your Perception

An event or an idea has no inherent ability to influence your emotional state. What causes emotions is your interpretation of an experience or notion. This explains why two individuals might have wildly different reactions to the same experience. One will see a problem and place the blame on external conditions, whilst the other will perceive an opportunity to seize. One will become immobile, while the other will expand.

Your interpretation of events is inextricably related to your broad ideas about life. As such, it is critical that we first examine the assumptions that underpin these interpretations.

Examining your premises

You established certain assumptions about how things should be in order to reach a certain emotional state. Your subjective world is defined by these assumptions. You do not dispute them since you are persuaded they are true.

The following are some instances of possible assumptions:

Issues should be avoided. This is an issue.

I should be in good health and expect to live at least until the age of seventy. I must marry. Complaining is quite natural.

There is nothing wrong with reflecting on the past, but I need to be concerned about the future, and/or I cannot be happy until or until I *insert your response(s) here*.

Now, let us examine each of these assumptions in turn:

The following issues should be avoided: Many individuals want to be free of their difficulties. However, what if you are unable to do so, or if you are not required to? Certain individuals have 'worse' difficulties than others, yet everyone has problems. What if the assumption that you should be trouble-free is incorrect? What if you're required to learn how to dance in the rain and make the most of your circumstances? What if difficulties are just obstacles to overcome—and a natural part of life?

This is an issue: What if the item you've labeled an issue isn't a problem at all? What if it isn't as critical as you believe? What if this is a disguised opportunity? And how would you do this?

I should be in good health: We often take our health for granted, yet there is no assurance that we will not get ill tomorrow. What if your health is a gift and not the default state? Wouldn't it alter your perspective on health?

I want to live at least until the age of seventy: You certainly anticipate living a long life, but what if this is not the case? Isn't having a long life a gift rather than a given? Regrettably, some individuals die at an early age, but such is the nature of reality. "He died too young," some say, but is that accurate? Isn't it more truthful to state he died recently? Neither excessively youthful nor excessively elderly.

I need to marry. Perhaps, perhaps not. That is entirely up to your interpretation. 'Shoulds' are often actions that society or your parents want you to do, although this does not have to be the case. Often, they are cultural standards or learned practices.

Complaining is quite natural: The majority of whining is an exercise in ego and is not useful. It serves no purpose and makes no difference. It serves no use other than to bolster your ego and annoy others. Attempt to go a complete week without complaining and see the results.

There is nothing improper in reminiscing about the past: You probably spend an inordinate amount of time ruminating about the past. Every single person does. However, are you aware that the past lives just in your mind? And are you aware that no matter what you do, you cannot alter it? While it is beneficial to learn from your history, focusing on it is not.

I'm obligated to be concerned about the future: While worrying about the future is inevitable to some level, it does not assist. Rather than that, you should do all possible in the present to prevent future difficulties.

I cannot be content till and until *insert your response(s)*: You do not have to live an ideal life to be happy. Every day, you must choose happiness. You must practice it since, as previously said, external things have little effect on your pleasure.

These are only a few instances of possible assumptions. My goal here is to demonstrate that your interpretations—and the feelings they generate—are primarily determined by the worldview you inhabit. Thus, it is critical that you spend time correcting your assumptions in order to experience more good feelings.

Conducting an examination of your interpretations

As previously said, you interpret occurrences according to your preconceptions. Now, the following questions will assist you in comprehending what I mean by interpretations.

- Do you believe that everything occurs for a purpose and that you should accept it, or do you prefer to play the victim?
- Do you think that momentary failures are only stepping stones on the path to success, or do you give up after your first severe setback?
- Do you make an attempt to alter things that are unchangeable or do you accept them?

- Do you feel you were sent on this earth for a reason, or do you drift through life with no discernible purpose?
- Are you of the belief that troubles are bad and should be avoided, or are you of the belief that they are an inevitable part of life?

Remember, what separates those who live happy lives from others who live sad ones are often how they perceive their experiences.

Taking action

Make a list of your emotional interpretations:

- You presently have one or two emotional difficulties. (Ask yourself, "If I could eliminate certain emotions, which ones would have the most beneficial effect on my life?")
- Your take on these problems. (Ask yourself, "What would I have to believe to believe my story?")
- New powerful interpretations to assist you in resolving these difficulties (Consider the following: What do I need to think in order to prevent feeling these bad emotions?)

Emotional Release

As previously shown, interpretation, identification, and repetition may all contribute to the development of powerful emotions. In this part, we'll examine how you might begin letting go of emotions that are impeding your progress toward the life you want.

Emotions are energy in action, but what happens when the energy is not allowed to move? It builds up. By suppressing your emotions, you are interfering with the natural flow of energy.

Unfortunately, no one taught you how to manage your emotions or that both pleasant and negative feelings are normal. Rather than that, they advised you to suppress your unpleasant feelings since they are harmful.

As a consequence, you may have spent years suppressing your feelings. By doing so, you enable them to penetrate further into your subconscious, eventually becoming an integral part of your identity. They have often developed into patterns that you may be unaware of. Perhaps you believe you are not good enough.

Or

Perhaps you suffer from guilt on a regular basis. These are the outcomes of long-held basic beliefs that you established via repression of your emotions.

The majority of us carries far too much emotional baggage and must learn to let it go. We need to clear our mind and eliminate the bad feelings that keep us from fully enjoying life.

The reality is that your subconscious mind is already trained to assist you in navigating life. Among other things, your subconscious ensures that you don't forget to breathe, keeps your heart pumping, and maintains your body temperature. It does not need extra beliefs in order to perform properly. Likewise, it is not required to 'store' feelings.

If you're like the majority of individuals, you spend the bulk of your time thinking. As a consequence, you're mostly disconnected from your emotions. To begin letting go of your emotions, you must first become aware of them by developing a stronger connection with your body and feelings.

The following are some simple measures you may take to begin letting go of your emotions.

1. Maintain a detached observation of your feelings.

Whenever you are confronted with a bad feeling, just observe it as objectively as possible. This entails reconnecting with your body. Recognize that each concept or picture that passes through your mind is not the feeling, but rather your perception of it. Experiment with sensing how it feels. Make an attempt to pinpoint the feeling. Consider how you would explain the feeling to another person. Bear in mind that:

Engage in a tale centered on that feeling, and believe in whatever pictures or ideas occur as a result of that experience.

2. Give your feeling a name

Bear in mind that emotions are only transient experiences, or, if you prefer, temporary garments. They are not referred to as 'you.'

When you feel an emotion, you express it using phrases such as "I am furious," "I am sad," or "I am depressed." Take note of how easily you relate with your feelings. This, however, is a factually false statement. Your emotions have nothing to do with who you really are. If you were your depression, you would be depressed 24 hours a day, every day of your life. That is not the case, fortunately.

Assume you are depressed. Rather of expressing, "I'm sad," a more appropriate approach to express that emotion is to say, "I feel sad" or "I have a sense of melancholy."

Can you see how this is distinct from just expressing, "I'm sad?" It provides you with more room to disengage from your emotions. The more conscious you become of your emotions, the simpler it will be to categorize and detach from them, and the easier it will be to let go of them.

3. Release your feelings

You often over-identify with and cling to your emotions for the following reasons:

They are a component of the narrative you are creating for yourself. At times, you can't help but cling to a tale, even if it's disempowering. Yes, you may develop an addiction to damaging tales despite the fact that they are detrimental to your well-being.

You think your emotions are who you are and have an intense desire to identify with them. You may fall into the delusion that you are your emotions. As a consequence, you develop a strong affinity for them, which results in anguish.

Real-world example: I often felt inadequate. As a consequence, I came to feel that I needed to work harder. This conviction prompted me to make daily to-do lists.

Even if you labor from daylight to night, this task is difficult to finish. I often fell short of my ambitions, reinforcing the feeling that I was unworthy.

By recognizing that this was really a tale, I began to let go of this notion. After doing so, I discovered that I was really doing almost as much work but without having to strain or feel pressured. I'm still working on that problem, but this approach has provided me with amazing value.

The difficult part was letting go of my story's connection by letting go of the following:

- The conviction that I am insufficient and must try harder
- The satisfaction I get from working harder than the majority of others
- The victim mindset that develops from working diligently but not achieving the desired goals
- The notion that I am somehow 'exceptional'
- The belief that the world requires change and the desire to exert control over the consequence of my activities.

As you can see, it is not simple to let go of fundamental feelings. They've been ingrained in our identity, and they often provide us with perverted pleasure. We may even ponder who we would be in the absence of them.

4. A five-step procedure for releasing emotions

Hale Dwoskin argues in his book, The Sedona Method, that there are three distinct methods for releasing your emotions as they emerge. You are able to:

1. Allow them to go. When you are confronted with bad emotions, you have the option of intentionally releasing them rather than

suppressing or clinging to them.

2. Give them permission to be here. You may either allow them by recognizing their presence while remaining apart from them, or you can

3. Greet them. You may accept them and examine them more closely to ascertain the source of these feelings.

Hale Dwoskin suggests that the first step in any circumstance is to become conscious of your emotions as they emerge. He then walks you through a five-step procedure for releasing your emotions:

Step 1: Concentrate on a certain feeling you'd want to focus on in order to feel better. This does not have to be a 'significant' feeling. It might be as easy as feeling uninspired to focus on a certain activity or being moderately irritated by something.

Step 2: Inquire about one of the following:

1. Could I let go of this sensation?

2. Could I allow this sensation to exist?

3. Could I accept this sensation?

Answer the relevant question based on your desired outcome (release, allow, or welcome).

Step 3: Then consider the question, "Would I?"

1. Would I be willing to let go of this sensation?

2. Would I let this sensation to exist?

3. Would I embrace this sensation?

Answer truthfully to each question with a yes or no. Do you believe you are capable of letting go/allowing/welcoming the emotion? Even a 'no' can assist you in letting go.

Your response will be, "Immediately." You quickly let go of that feeling.

You could dismiss this strategy as over simplistic and ineffectual. That is not acceptable! Consider it for yourself. Always keep in mind that you are not your feelings. That is exactly how you will learn to let go of them.

Acknowledge this global reality. As you consciously choose to let go of your emotions, embrace them completely, or just allow them to be, you'll receive a fresh perspective on how emotions function and how to release them.

Create a list of all the feelings you want to release. Perhaps you feel insufficient. Perhaps you suffer from procrastination and are filled with guilt and humiliation. Perhaps you're blaming yourself for something you've done in the past, or you're concerned about the future. Simply jot down whatever comes to mind. Now, use the aforementioned procedure.

Choose one feeling and then consider the following:

- "Could I let go of this sensation?" "Would I do that?" (Yes/no) "When?" (Now)

- Don't worry if you're not successful at first.
- You'll have lots of practice chances in the future.

Conditionalizing Your Mind To Enjoy More Positive Emotions

To regain control of your emotions, it's critical to understand how your ideas contribute to the generation of emotions in general. Your ideas elicit specific emotions, which in turn produce further thoughts. Then, thoughts and emotions feed off one another.

For example, if the belief "I'm not good enough" is believed, unpleasant feelings such as shame or guilt would result. On the other hand, when you are embarrassed of your 'inadequacy,' you will attract additional ideas that support that attitude. You'll concentrate on the things (you feel) you're not excellent at, or you'll recall and linger on previous failures. This reinforces your erroneous view.

Emotions are generated by thoughts, and emotions control your actions. If you believe you do not deserve a promotion, you will not request one. If you feel a guy or woman is 'out of your league,' you will refrain from approaching him or her.

This is, in a nutshell, how thoughts function. They elicit emotions, which influence your behavior and form your world. While this may not be immediately apparent, with time, you will understand that your ideas have a significant influence on your life.

Your future is determined by your thoughts and emotions.

Humans possess a quality that no other living being possesses: imagination. We may materialize things with our thoughts and transform the unseen into the apparent.

However, a thought alone is insufficient to materialize objects or conditions. It must be fed by emotional energy; such as zeal, excitement, passion, or joy. As a result, someone who is excited about his or her ambition will accomplish more than someone who is gloomy and uninspired.

Successful individuals are always focused on what they want with a positive outlook, while failed people are continually focused on what they do not desire or lack. The latter are fearful of running out of money, skill, time, or any other resource necessary to accomplish their objectives. As a consequence, pessimists achieve far less than they are capable of.

As a result, one of the most critical abilities you may develop is the capacity to manage your thoughts and emotions. This requires a grasp of what emotions are, how they operate, and why they exist. Later, we'll cover how to harness the power of your emotions for personal development.

Creating a bank of good ideas in your head

Each day, confident individuals put pleasant ideas into their brains. They rejoice in minor victories and treat themselves with kindness and respect. Naturally, people anticipate positive outcomes. On the other side, individuals with low self-esteem constantly assault their minds with notions that are disempowering. They dismiss their successes as 'insignificant' and fail to acknowledge their own talents and the good purpose that motivated their activities. It's understandable that they feel unworthy.

Both use their minds to alter reality, but who do you believe is better off? Who is the more optimistic thinker, or the more negative thinker?

Does this imply that positive thinking will fix all your difficulties and permanently eradicate your bad emotions? Obviously not. Thought manipulation is only one of the methods available to help you get control of your emotions.

The bounds of optimistic thought

Repeating "I'm happy, I'm happy, I'm happy" to yourself all day will not transform you into a living Buddha. You may gain from it, but you will continue to suffer bad emotions as a result of it. Unless you understand how to manage unpleasant emotions when they arise, you will become a victim of your own disempowering tale. This narrative might be the reason you're such a failure or the reason why *insert your favorite disempowering story here*.

Interestingly, individuals are often attached to their story—even bad ones—and unwilling to let go of the 'why', for the following reasons:

Are intrinsically defective

Will never be happy because they *insert favorite tale here* are not deserving of love

Are never going to succeed, and are never going to marry, and so on.

I'm certain you're hooked to a narrative. Now, we'll talk about how to train your mind to feel more happy emotions. Following that, we'll examine your ability to cope with unpleasant emotions when they come.

To begin conditioning your mind, choose the emotion(s) you want to feel more of. Do you want happiness? Are you more motivated? Are you more proactive? The second stage is to implement a customized program that will enable you to feel your desired emotion (s). The third stage is to regularly practice experiencing that emotion.

Repetition of the same feeling enables you to more easily access it. Neuroscience has shown that frequently encountering the same idea or emotion strengthens the associated brain circuits, facilitating future access to that concept or emotion. Simply said, the more times you encounter a feeling, the simpler it is to produce. That is when everyday conditioning enters the picture.

To train your mind to perceive happy emotions, you may follow the steps outlined previously:

Interpretation + identification + repetition = strong emotion

Here is how to use the formula in this situation:

Interpretation: Visualizing certain events or ideas that you see as favorable.

Identification: Feeling the way you wish to feel in response to these experiences or ideas. This may be accomplished by using any of the approaches discussed in the section 'What affects your emotions,' such as positive affirmations and visualization.

Repetition: Continue repeating and associating with the same concepts. By doing so, you enable your mind to more quickly access the associated emotions.

The following are some examples of methods you may employ to achieve the desired state of mind:

1. Gratitude

Make appreciation a daily habit to increase your gratitude. Each morning, take a moment to reflect on what you are thankful for. The more you practice, the more adept you will be at focusing on the good. Unfortunately, the majority of us are aware that we should be thankful, yet we are not. That is why we must nurture an attitude of thankfulness. As the late Jim Rohn put it, "our emotions must be educated just as much as our brains."

The following activities can help you create an attitude of gratitude:

A. Make a list of things for which you are grateful: Take a pen and paper, or better yet, a dedicated notebook, and jot down at least three things for which you are thankful. This will assist you in focusing on the good aspects of life.

B. Express gratitude to those who have touched your life: Close your eyes and consider the individuals you've met. As you see them one by one, express gratitude and acknowledge at least one wonderful thing they done for you. If you chance to see someone you dislike, express your gratitude and search for one nice thing they did for you. It might be for the purpose of strengthening you or teaching you a certain lesson. Rather of attempting to control your thoughts, just allow familiar faces to come to mind. Release whatever animosity you are experiencing or have experienced.

C. Concentrate on a single thing and be grateful for its existence:

Consider one thing in your room and consider the amount of effort and the number of individuals involved in its creation and delivery to you. Consider the labor involved in creating a chair, for example. Some were tasked with designing it, while others were tasked with locating raw materials and assembling it. It had to be delivered to the store by truck drivers. The personnel at the business were required to exhibit and promote it. You or another individual was required to gather it. Additionally, the automobile you drive has to be constructed by others, and so on.

Consider how this chair benefits you: Consider a moment when you were so exhausted that you couldn't wait to sit. Wasn't it wonderful to finally be able to sit? Not only can you sit on the chair, but you can also use it to type, read, sip coffee, or just have a good chat with your friends.

D. Gratitude song/guided meditation: Listen to a gratitude song or guided meditation.

2. Excitement

At times, you may experience a loss of enthusiasm. You're locked in the same old pattern and feel as though you're running in circles. To increase your enthusiasm, spend a few minutes each morning imagining all you want. Be ecstatic about these matters. The following are numerous methods for doing so (please note that this should be done on a regular basis):

A. Make a list of what you desire: Take a pen and a piece of paper and write at the top of the page, 'What I Want.' Then, jot down everything that intrigues you.

B. Visualize the outcome you desire: Consider the question, "What do I really want?" and envision all the things you desire. Make an attempt to be as descriptive as possible. Clarity is a virtue. Consider your ideal job, relationship, or lifestyle, as well as any aspirations you have for the next decade or beyond.

C. Keep a notebook of your aims and dreams: Purchase a notepad and jot down your life objectives in each category. Each morning, go through them and continue to add photographs, sketches, or anything else that may help you maintain your passion.

D. Visualize your dream day vividly:

- What kind of breakfast would you eat?
- What would you do with your day?
- Whom would you choose to spend your day with?
- How would you spend your evenings?
- Where would you choose to live?
- What would your reaction be?

Your perfect day might take on a variety of forms. Simply ensure that each variation thrills you.

3. Confidence/certainty

If you want to boost your confidence in your capacity to accomplish your objectives, imagine yourself already having done so and feeling good about it. Develop a feeling of assurance via practice. Commit to your mental picture. Each time you picture your objective, commit to it with your energy. Recognize that it will occur.

4. Self-esteem

Keep note of your everyday successes to increase your self-esteem. You do a lot of things correctly, but you tend to recall only the things you do incorrectly. It's unsurprising that your self-esteem declines. Purchase a notepad and set it aside for this purpose. Each day, keep track of your successes. Several instances of achievements include the following:

I awoke promptly. I ate some fruit, tidied my desk, accomplished Project A, exercised, and/or read.

As you can see, you are not required to write anything significant. Indeed, by documenting little victories, you train your mind to seek out other victories, which gradually improves your self-esteem.

For further self-esteem activities, see the section 'Not feeling good enough.'

5. Decisiveness

As you develop greater decisiveness, your productivity will increase, which will have a positive effect on your well-being. As we will see in the section on 'Procrastination,' delaying may result in significant mental distress.

To increase your decisiveness, you might use Mel Robbins' 5 second Rule, which she established in her book of the same name. Mel Robbins claims in it that there is just one rule for productivity, success, and obtaining everything you've ever desired: you must do something regardless of how you feel. If you're willing to do the things you're not in the mood to accomplish, you'll get all you've ever desired.

According to her 5 Second Rules, you have five seconds from the time you conceive an idea until the time you act. If you do not act in these five seconds, your mind will convince you otherwise. The mind's tendency is to keep us from undertaking anything frightening or exhausting. For instance, you have five seconds to do the following:

Introduce yourself to someone you're interested in speaking with during an event. Send that critical e-mail, or

During a meeting, pose a question.

Strengthen your decisiveness via exercise

To begin practicing the 5 Second Rule, begin with modest tasks.

Make a list of the factors that cause you to postpone. Perhaps you have put off dishwashing or cleaning your house. Perhaps you put off phoning someone or sending an email. Make a note of it.

Now, choose a few items for which you will use the 5 Second Rule. Make a commitment to following the rule for at least one week. When you consider doing the dishes, phoning someone, or *insert desired task*, count down from five to zero and act before you reach zero.

Common errors to avoid while programming your mind include the following.

Avoid the following blunders when you train your mind to feel more happy emotions:

Attempting to apply an excessive number of changes concurrently: Concentrate on one or two exercises for about a month before attempting others.

Starting too large: Begin small and ensure that the workouts are not too difficult. Bear in mind that regaining control of your emotions is a long-term endeavor. This is not a sprint, but a marathon.

How to Modify Your Feelings by Modifying Your Actions

As previously shown, you may control your emotions by the use of your body, intellect, or speech. Additionally, we covered how you might alter your emotional state by altering your perceptions of things or experiences. Unfortunately, when negative emotions surface unexpectedly or become too powerful, just altering your body position or employing positive affirmation may not be sufficient. Indeed, attempts to overcome a bad mood with a more pleasant one often fail. You cannot always conquer sadness by cheering yourself up or alleviate sorrow by just choosing to 'feel happy.' Similarly, you cannot expect intense pain to vanish by repeatedly repeating the phrase/mantra, "I'm happy, I'm happy, I'm happy."

You can, however, change how you feel by altering your conduct. Your sentiments will shift in lockstep with your conduct. It may occur nearly instantly, like when you complete an activity to divert your attention away from moderate rage. Alternatively, it may take weeks or even months while you work through deep feelings such as sadness or despair.

To begin altering your emotional state, anytime you are confronted with a bad feeling, ask yourself the following questions:

- "What is the source of that emotion?" and
- "How can I change my current reality?"

Following these inquiries, identify specific activities you may do to alter your mental state.

Bear in mind that emotions, by their very nature, dissipate with time. That is, unless you reinforce them by mentally repeating the same incident over. The following are some real-world examples to help you see how it works:

Example 1: If you continue to recall the wonderful moments you had together with grief after your boyfriend or girlfriend broke up with you, it will take longer to recover from the break-up. While there is nothing wrong with being sad or recalling the past, if you wish to move on, it is preferable to avoid rehashing the past whenever feasible. In this scenario, modifying your behavior would include making a concerted effort to avoid reliving past memories.

Example 2: If you are continually concerned about an impending presentation at work, modifying your behavior may be as time-consuming as hours spent memorizing your speech. By doing so, you will get so familiar with the material that you will be able to perform effectively under duress. To increase your chances of success even more, you might even practice in front of your coworkers or acquaintances.

Example 3: If you've been resentful of a certain buddy for weeks over something he said or did, one way to change your behavior is to have an honest conversation with him and express your thoughts. This will enable you to clear the air and resolve any disputes.

Misconceptions and avert the development of anger. Frequently, we misread situations or see things that are not there.

Example 4: There are moments when you feel unhappy, angry, or even depressed and are unable to change your feelings. In this case, the best course of action is to avoid concentrating on your emotions and just let them to be. Your task here is to carry out your responsibilities and live your life till these feelings subside. Remember to practice releasing unpleasant feelings as they emerge. As you develop the ability to disassociate from unpleasant feelings, you will be able to prevent them from expanding and becoming more entrenched.

A Change in Your Environment Can Change Emotions

Your emotions are not always within your control. Certain situations, such as a breakup, the death of a loved one, or the diagnosis of a serious illness, might elicit unpleasant feelings.

You do, however, have some power over some occurrences. Do you face everyday living challenges that jeopardize your mental health? What if you could take action against them?

Oftentimes, the simplest way to alleviate bad feelings is to avoid the conditions that generate them in the first place. Perhaps you watch too much television, which contributes to your misery. Or maybe seeing your (apparently) happy pals on Facebook makes you feel like a failure. Why not spend less time in these instances?

Real-world illustration:

Facebook was causing me distress and making me feel inadequate. People in my industry were crushing it, and my buddies seemed to be ecstatic (or so I thought). Not to mention how much time I was squandering idly browsing through my newsfeed. To compensate for this drain on my emotional 'bank,' I dramatically limited my Facebook use. I've been feeling better ever since I made the choice.

This example demonstrates how modest adjustments may significantly improve your well-being. If you examine your everyday activities, you will discover activities or behaviors that do not contribute to your pleasure. Simply discontinuing one or two of these hobbies, or altering some habits, may significantly enhance your mood.

You may already be aware of what you should do, but you may be uninformed of the cost of certain habits to your well-being.

I've included some instances below of activities or habits that may sap your pleasure. Consider if they add to your overall feeling of well-being:

While watching television might be enjoyable, it is also a passive pastime that may not add much to your pleasure.

Social networking is easy and helps you to stay connected with your pals, but it can also be addicting. Facebook or Twitter may transform you into an addict seeking external validation.

Associating with bad people: The people you associate with have a significant impact on your emotional condition. Positive individuals will encourage you and assist you in realizing your greatest aspirations. Negative individuals drain your energy, demotivate you, and suffocate your potential. "You are the average of the five people with whom you spend the most time," Jim Rohn once stated. Assemble the proper group of individuals around you.

Complaining and concentrating only on the negative: Do you continually focus on the bad aspects of situations? Are you a victim of your own reminiscences? If this is the case, what effect does this have on your level of happiness?

Not completing what you begin: In both your personal and professional life, leaving jobs and projects incomplete may have a negative influence on your mood. Your mind becomes cluttered with unfinished business. Feeling overwhelmed or demotivated is an indication that your life may include too many 'open loops.' Examples of 'open loops' include incomplete work for which you have been delaying or avoiding persons with whom you need to communicate.

These are only a few examples. And how about you? Which hobbies or habits deprive you of happiness?

Solutions for dealing with negative emotions in the short and long term are available

To help you better cope with unpleasant emotions, I've compiled a list of exercises and approaches. Your future will be filled with a variety of bad feelings, ranging from moderate annoyance to sadness, no matter how much mental control you have. You'll need to be ready.

I've included both long-term and short-term options for dealing with unpleasant emotions below.

First, short-term fixes

The following methods will assist you in coping with bad feelings. Keep the ones that work for you.

A. Change your emotional state

It's just as powerful as you allow it to be, so distract yourself. Instead than dwelling on a bad emotion, go to work straight away. Take something off your to-do list to vent your frustration. Do something that takes your whole concentration if feasible.

Do something outlandish to disrupt the flow of the conversation. Don't be afraid to yell, dance, or talk in an odd voice.

Stand up, take a stroll, perform push-ups, dance, or utilize a powerful posture to get your heart racing. By altering your physical state, you may alter your emotional state.

Your emotional state may be affected by listening to your favorite music.

Give yourself a pep talk by shouting at yourself with an authoritative tone. Emotions may be changed through speaking and writing.

B. Take a step forward

Don't be afraid to do it: Do what you need to do, regardless of how you feel about it. Regardless of how they feel about it, mature folks do what they have to do.

It's time to take action: Feelings are influenced by your actions. Take a moment to ask yourself, "What can I do today that will help me feel better?" You should next proceed to carry out such action.

C. Pay attention to your feelings

Write down what you're worried about, why you're concerned, and the steps you can take to alleviate your concerns. Attempt to be as descriptive as you can.

Make a record of what occurred: Write down the actual events that caused you to feel the way you do. Avoid writing down your personal version of it or the drama that surrounded it. Write down the facts as they are, without any embellishment or embellishment. Now ask yourself whether it's truly that important in the larger picture of your life.

Talk: Have a conversation with a fellow human being. It's possible that you're overreacting and exaggerating the situation. There are times when you just have to look at things from a new angle.

Remember a point in your life when you felt good about yourself: This might help you go back to that condition and develop a fresh outlook. The following questions to ask yourself are "How did it feel?" How did I get myself into this situation? How did I feel about life back then?

Allow yourself to feel what you're feeling: Ask yourself, "Am I capable of letting that feeling go?" Then, allow yourself to let go of it.

Emotions should be allowed to flow: Put an end to your attempts to control or suppress your feelings. Let them be who they naturally are.

Embody your feelings: Stay true to yourself. Observe them as closely as you can while maintaining your distance.

Become interested in them. What do they really stand for at the heart of their being?

D. Take it easy

Take some time to yourself and relax. Negative emotions are more likely to surface when you're weary than when you're well rested.

Slowly inhale and exhale. Your emotional state is influenced by your breathing. Breathing exercises may help you relax or rev up your vitality.

Relax your muscles for a few minutes. Begin by letting go of the tension in your jaw, the area surrounding your eyes, and the facial muscles. Your body impacts your emotions. As you relax your body, your mind also relaxes.

Bless your problems: Thank your issues. Understand they are here for a purpose and will serve you in some manner.

2. Long-term solutions

The following approaches can help you control your negative emotions long-term.

A. Analyze your unpleasant feelings

Identify the narrative behind your feelings: Take a pen and paper, and write down all the reasons why you have these emotions in the first place. What assumptions do you hold? How did you understand what's occurring to you? Now, check if you can let go of this specific narrative.

Write down your feelings in a journal: Take a few minutes each day to jot down how you feel. Look for repeating trends. Then, utilize affirmations, visualization, or an appropriate activity to assist you overcomes these feelings.

Practice mindfulness: Observe your emotions throughout the day. Meditation will help you achieve this. Another technique is just to participate in an activity while being completely present. As you're doing this, notice what's going on in your head.

B. Move away from negativity

Alter environment: If you're surrounded by negativity, change your surroundings. Move to a new area, or limit the time you spend with negative people.

Remove unhelpful activities: Remove or minimize the time you spend on any activity not having a beneficial influence on your life. This may be lowering the time you spend watching TV or perusing the internet.

C. Condition your thoughts

Create everyday rituals: This will allow you to feel more good emotions. Meditate, exercise, repeat affirmations, make a gratitude diary, and so forth. (The greatest time to deposit happy ideas in your mind is shortly before going to sleep and first thing in the morning.)

Exercise: Exercise frequently. Exercise increases your mood and is helpful for your emotional and physical wellbeing.

D. Increase your energy

The less energy you have, the more prone you are to feel unpleasant emotions.

Improve your sleep: Make sure you get adequate sleep. If feasible, go to bed and wake up at the same time every day.

Eat healthier food: As the phrase goes, "You are what you eat." Junk food can adversely affect your energy levels, so take efforts to enhance your diet.

Rest: Take frequent naps, or take a few minutes to rest Breathe: Learn to breathe correctly.

E. Ask for aid

Visit a professional: if you have severe emotional concerns such as very low self-esteem or depression, it could be beneficial to consult a specialist.

PART IV

Introducing Yourself To Emotional Growth

We've discussed what emotions are, how they're produced, and how you can rewire your brain to have more pleasant ones. Now, let's look at how you might harness your emotions for personal development.

The majority of individuals underestimate the value of emotions. They are never completely aware that their emotions may be used to develop.

Consider the following. Your emotions are communicating with you. They inform you that your existing view of reality is skewed. The issue is never with reality, but with your interpretation of it. Never forget that you have the ability to discover significance and pleasure even in the most difficult circumstances.

Alice Sommer, for example, had every cause to despair. During WWII, she was imprisoned in a concentration camp and had no idea how much longer she had to live. Despite this, she discovered pleasure. . As she recalls:

I was always laughing. We were lying on the floor with my son, and he saw me laughing. How can a child not laugh when the mother laughs?

— AlICE SOMMER

Nick Vujicic believed he would never be happy. After all, he was born with no arms or legs. As he said in one of the lectures he gave at a school, What kind of husband am I gonna be if I can't even hold my wife's hand?

— NICK VUJICIC

Nobody would have faulted him if he had stayed resentful his whole life under these circumstances. He overcame his obstacles and is now a successful motivational speaker, as well as a loving husband and father of two.

These two instances demonstrate that we can overcome even the most difficult circumstances. They demonstrate that unpleasant feelings do not stay indefinitely. Challenging situations in our lives are often the catalysts for our growth as human beings. Even a full mental breakdown has the potential to act as a wake-up call for individuals.

This part will teach you how emotions function and how to harness their power to help you develop while also alleviating the emotional misery they cause.

Introducing the Power of Emotions In Your Life

Emotions come and go and, in the end, are incapable of defining you. However, this does not negate their importance. They may help you develop personally by reiterating what you already know: you must make adjustments in your life. The more you deny your feelings, the more outspoken they become. It all begins with a quiet whisper, a gut instinct, or intuitive knowing. As you ignore this sign, it becomes more loud. Continue to ignore your emotions, and your body will begin to communicate in the same manner that physical pain does.

For instance, suppose you experience a feeling you label 'stress.' This indicates that you should make some adjustments in your life. It may include removing yourself from a stressful situation, fixing the issue, or altering your perception of it. One thing is certain: you must take action. If you continue to ignore stress or the stressor, you risk developing serious health problems.

The basic line is that your emotions communicate with you. Similarly to how physical pain indicates that something is wrong with your body, mental distress indicates that something is wrong with your mind.

Self-transformative awareness's power

Self-awareness is a critical component of personal development. Without it, you will be unable to make significant changes in your life, since you cannot address an issue before you recognize it exists.

Thus, what exactly is self-awareness? Self-awareness is the capacity to watch your thoughts, feelings, and actions objectively, without interjecting your own interpretation or tale.

Is it better to be above or below the line?

Jim Dethmer and Diana Chapman created a very basic but effective paradigm for increasing self-awareness in The 15 Commitments of Conscious Leadership. This model is exceedingly straightforward: it consists just a single line. The authors contend that you are either above or below the line at any given moment. While you're above the line, you're receptive, interested, and eager to learn; when you're below the line, you're defensive and resistant to new ideas. Simply said, you are awake while you are above the line and unconscious when you are below the line.

Whichever side of the line you are on is determined by your emotional state. When you perceive a danger to your physical life or to your ego, you cross the line and attempt to defend yourself in order to ensure your survival (or that of your ego). On the other hand, when you operate above the law, you are in a good mood. Your originality, creativity, and teamwork are all at their peak, resulting in increased performance.

Your capacity to detect when you have over the boundary significantly influences your ability to regulate your emotional state. You cannot alter a feeling if you are unaware of its existence. This is what it means to be 'aware' or 'conscious. The following are some instances of actions that are 'above the line' and 'below the line.'

You are: Inquisitive above the line

- Conscious listening Sensitization to emotions
- Without being argumentative, discussing Appreciating
- Accepting accountability, and
- Putting your views into question.
- Adhering to a position
- Identifying flaws
- Arguing
- Justifying and rationalizing Gossiping

Recruiting people to reaffirm your convictions, and Assault on the messenger.

Contrary to fear, there is also a conflict between love and fear.

Another straightforward approach is the Fear vs. Love Model. Throughout the day, you behave out of either fear or love. When your primary goal is to get anything, whether it is another person's praise or attention, money or power, you behave out of fear. When you behave out of love, on the other hand, your primary emphasis is on giving, whether it's your time, money, affection, or attention. You desire to share and enhance the lives of others around you just for the sake of it.

While your behaviors may reflect both a want to give and a desire to receive, one of these components is often more evident. To manage your emotions, you must first learn to distinguish between acts of love and acts of fear. Consider one of your primary life objectives. Is it a fear-based or a love-based objective? Are you attempting to contribute and offer to the world, or are you attempting to take from it?

For instance, suppose you want to pursue a career as an actress. Several explanations for this might include the following:

1. Earning money

2. Becoming famous

3. Demonstrating to your parents and friends that you are capable

4. Entertaining people

5. Self-expression

The first three examples are often fear-based behaviors: you desire to show your competence and fill a gap inside yourself. The last two examples are acts of love that emphasize a desire to share your talent with the world.

As we explain how various emotions function in more detail, keep these two models in mind: above/below the line and fear-based vs. love-based acts.

Take note that during the day, you often shift between acts motivated by love and those motivated by fear. For instance, you may get involved in an activity that benefits others and gives you a sense of accomplishment. You need nothing at the time. You can picture how delighted your father will be five minutes later when you finally win a promotion. You are no longer whole in this moment. Rather than that, you're attempting to get something (in this case, your father's approval).

Begin to become aware of the underlying motives behind your behaviors. As you do so, you'll notice how much time you waste attempting to win the approval of others, whether it's your colleague, your employer, your parents, or your spouse. Take note of this and consider what you can do to shift your focus from 'wanting to gain' to 'wanting to give.'

With these two models in mind, let's look at how you might increase your awareness of the emotions you encounter on a daily basis.

A Record of Your Feelings

The first step in improving your emotional well-being is to increase your awareness of the emotions you encounter on a daily basis. Before you can begin to develop more happy feelings, you must first establish a baseline.

To shed light on the feelings you encounter on a daily basis, I ask you to keep a journal of your emotions for a complete week. To do so, use a notepad or the attached worksheet. Spend a few minutes each day recording how you feel and rating yourself on a scale of 1 to 10, with 1 being the worst possible feeling and 10 representing the greatest possible feeling. Give yourself an overall score at the conclusion of the week and answer the following questions: -

- ✓ What unpleasant feelings did you experience?
- ✓ What elicited these feelings?
- ✓ What are the unambiguous facts?
- ✓ Did you have particular ideas that contributed to your feelings?
- ✓ Were these unfavorable feelings triggered by external events?
- ✓ Have you been deprived of sleep?
- ✓ Have you fallen ill?
- ✓ Have you been involved in an accident?
- ✓ What really occurred? (Not in your thoughts, but in reality)
- ✓ How did you perceive the facts?
- ✓ What are you need to believe in order to feel that way?
- ✓ Are your beliefs valid?
- ✓ Could you have felt better by having a different interpretation of ideas or events?
- ✓ How did you revert to a condition of neutrality?
- ✓ What occurred precisely?
- ✓ Have your ideas shifted?
- ✓ Have you taken action on the tasks you had been putting off?
- ✓ Was it a natural occurrence?
- ✓ How could you have avoided or mitigated these bad emotions?

Consider the following concrete example:

Assume you keep a weekly diary of your feelings and observe that you were somewhat depressed for a few of days. This is how it would look:

What was the source of this emotion?

At work, I was assigned a job and felt unable or incompetent to perform it.

What really occurred?

I was tasked with doing a task, which I accomplished.

How did you interpret the facts?

I had the impression that I was inept and that everyone else in the workplace could do the assignment but me.

I felt as if I should have been capable of successfully completing the work. I had the distinct impression that everyone was evaluating me.

What would you have to believe in order to have that feeling?

I'd have to believe:

I am inept.

Incompetence is intolerable.

I should have been capable of doing the duty. Everybody is evaluating me.

- ✓ Are your convictions valid?
- ✓ Are you really inept?

Perhaps I'm prejudiced and assessed myself too severely.

   ✓   Is incompetence considered acceptable?

No. The reality is that I am not always proficient in every area.

   ✓   Should you be capable of doing that task?

I lack experience completing such duties, and there was no way I could complete them without seeking assistance.

   ✓   Is it true that everyone has an opinion about you?

While some may condemn me, this is most likely not true of everyone. Additionally, it is conceivable that nobody cares. After all, they have their own concerns. And what happens if no one notices? Or maybe I performed well and the negative is all in my head.

   ✓   How did you revert to a condition of neutrality?

I realized it wasn't such a huge issue after all. I checked with a coworker to ensure that I completed the assignment appropriately. He aided me and counseled me. He also advised several books that would assist me in honing my talents.

   ✓   What might you have done differently to minimize or lessen the intensity of this bad emotion?

I could have asked for assistance rather than attempting to handle everything on my own.

As you go through this process, you will become aware of the factors that contribute to your bad feelings. You'll be able to recognize and overcome self-defeating tendencies via regular training and praise.

Additionally, consider the following:

Remember to journal about your feelings each day in a dedicated diary. This will assist you in detaching yourself from your emotions as you come to terms with the fact that ups and downs are a natural part of life.

Failure to Be Good Enough

Do you ever feel as though you're not good enough? What a surprise! You are not alone.

Whether you are aware of it or not, millions of individuals share your sentiments. The sense of 'not being good enough' must have put an end to more aspirations than anything else. And who hasn't felt that way at some point in their lives? The following is a partial (non-exhaustive) account of how I felt throughout my life:

- ✓ I am insufficiently talented as a writer, insufficiently personable, and insufficiently competent.
- ✓ I lack confidence.
- ✓ I lack the necessary guts. I lack sufficient self-discipline.
- ✓ I am insufficiently skilled at public speaking, and I am insufficiently gorgeous.
- ✓ I am insufficiently inspirational
- ✓ I am insufficiently interested
- ✓ I am not wealthy enough, and I am not muscular enough.
- ✓ I lack sufficient patience.

- ✓ I lack the necessary perseverance. I am insufficiently proactive.
- ✓ I am insufficiently productive. I am not intelligent enough
- ✓ I am not assertive enough; I am not tough enough.
- ✓ I am not working diligently enough. My English is inadequate.
- ✓ My Japanese is inadequate, and my memory is inadequate.

And I could go on indefinitely.

Individuals who believe they are not good enough often suffer from poor self-esteem. They concentrate on what they are not excellent at while ignoring what they are good at. If you attempt to complement them, all you will hear is, "It's no big deal." Worse, they may believe you're being courteous or attempting to influence them.

These individuals have a difficult difficulty receiving praise. Rather of just saying thank you, they either repay the praise or minimize their participation.

Perhaps you're doing similarly? Consider if you perform one of the following when you get a compliment:

1. Dismiss the whole incident as insignificant: "Anyone might have done it."

2. Discuss all of the things you did incorrectly while elaborating on what you might have done better.

3. Make an attempt to reciprocate the compliment: "Thank you. I believe you performed an excellent job as well.

Take note of your difficulty to take a praise completely in the three instances above.

You may not only gloss over your triumphs, but also accentuate each and every one of your failures to bolster the argument that you are unworthy. You maintain a lengthy record of your failures, hesitant to let them go because they suit your narrative. Who would you be if you weren't the always unsatisfactory guy or woman? As weird as it may seem, there is an element of fear in it. At the very least, the knowledge of not being good enough provides some solace.

Consider what would happen if you let go of your grip on your tale, attempted something you've always desired, and failed. What you've always thought would become true: you're not good enough. Or, much worse, what would happen if you succeeded? How does it fit into your narrative?

Bear in mind that your brain is predisposed to negativity. Adding your own prejudice will almost surely make you feel worse about yourself. The reality is that you excel at the majority of tasks. While a lack of experience, passion, or skill may explain why you aren't doing as well as you would want in some areas, it has nothing to do with your being 'insufficient'.

How to improve by using the emotion of not being good enough

Feeling insufficient is an indication of poor self-esteem. Numerous individuals suffer from varying degrees of poor self-esteem. Certainly, I do. For some, nothing they do is adequate. Others feel inadequate in certain circumstances or parts of their lives. Wherever you are on the self-esteem continuum, you may almost certainly benefit from a boost.

The first step is to ascertain what causes these emotions. Which of the following ideas do you identify with? Which spheres of your life are at stake?

Spend a few moments writing the following:

- ✓ Situations in which you feel inadequate, and
- ✓ The concepts with which you identify (your story).

Maintaining a record of your successes

The second stage is to maintain a record of your achievements. Not feeling good enough is often the consequence of a distorted picture of oneself. You are fixated on your flaws, oblivious to your accomplishments. Individuals with a strong self-esteem tend to see themselves objectively, accepting both their flaws and talents.

To boost your self-esteem, begin by recognizing all of the things you do well. The activities that follow will assist you in doing this.

Create a victory log in Exercise 1.

Writing down your successes is an excellent approach to do so. I recommend you to utilize your dedicated notepad for this activity.

1. To begin, make a list of all you've done in your life. Create a list of fifty items. If you run out of ideas, jot down lesser achievements. This will let you appreciate how far you've come.

2. At the conclusion of each day, jot down what you did. It might be anything as basic as:

I awoke on time, exercised, and had a nutritious breakfast.

Each day, attempt to generate five to ten new ideas.

Exercise 2: Restock your jar with self-esteem

Alternatively, you may keep track of your accomplishments by writing them down on different pieces of paper and storing them in a jar. Several advice follow to ensure that you get the most out of this exercise:

Ascertain that your jar (or any other container you employ) is visible. The optimal placement is almost certainly on your desk; the second-best option is probably in your bedroom.

Choose a container that appeals to you. Choose a design that appeals to you. It's all about your self-esteem, thus everything that boosts your confidence is recommended. Ascertain that it is transparent so that you can monitor the filling process.

Give it a favorable name (e.g. my self-esteem jar, declaration of love to myself etc.).

Write your achievement on a piece of paper that you like. For instance, choose a variety of colors so that when the jar is full, it makes a pleasing visual effect. One possibility is to utilize origami paper.

Utilize your preferred pen.

The goal is to increase your regard for yourself by recognizing your many successes.

Create a positive notebook as a third exercise.

Additionally, you may keep a notebook in which you can record every praise you get that day. If a coworker compliments you on your shoes, jot it down. If a buddy praised your hair, make a note of it. Your manager complimented you on your performance.

Additionally, jot down what you accomplished throughout a job. Make no mistake about the genuineness of these praises. Assume they are authentic at all times. The goal is to teach your mind to concentrate on the good events that occur in your life—events that occur regardless of whether you notice them. How to get the most out of the workout is as follows:

Purchase a notepad that you like.

Individualize it: Add stickers, draw anything, or use a variety of colors. You're not interested in doing any of this? That is OK as well. It is, after all, your diary.

Keep it on your person: Carry it about with you and keep an eye out for fresh compliments to add to your incredible collection (optional).

Every day, go over it: Go over previous postings and mentally express gratitude to those who have commended you. You may say, "I appreciate you, *insert name*." You are welcome to read previous posts in the morning, evening, or both (or whenever you feel like it). It is all up to you.

This, once again, is your journal. These are only recommendations. Whatever is most convenient for you?

Accepting praises

There is a good chance that you have difficulty receiving praises. Are the following phrases familiar to you:

It is never a significant event.

Each and every one of us could have done it.

That is why 'so and so' aided you. I could have done it more effectively.

Here is an excellent reason to accept compliments: because the person who offered the compliment wants for you to accept it, not for it to be flushed down the toilet! Consider that you recently gave someone a present. How would you feel if that individual dumped the present on the floor, walked on it, then tossed it away after opening the box? You're not going to like it, are you? Regrettably, it is often what we do when we get a praise; When we choose not to.

By refusing to accept a praise, we show contempt for the person who made the effort to provide it. Wouldn't it be nice to have your praise appreciated wholeheartedly?

Accept praises as a first exercise

This little activity can assist you in accepting a praise. When someone complements you, respond as follows:

I'd want to express my gratitude to *insert the individual's name*.

That is all. Nothing could be easier. No, "I appreciate you, but...", "I appreciate you, too," or "It wasn't a big deal." Simply express gratitude.

How to get the most out of the workout is as follows:

Extend a heartfelt thank you in a strong and clear voice. You may notice that you have a propensity to suppress your emotions and end up almost mechanically saying thank you. Indeed, you may discover that you've never really expressed your gratitude.

Provide time for it to sink in: Before beginning a new statement, allow room for the expression of thanks. Do not minimize the praise or explain why you are deserving (or undeserving) of it.

Express yourself authentically: Express your gratitude by conveying your sentiments to the individual who complemented you. You may encounter opposition. Many of us have difficulty expressing thanks, owing to our pride. After all, we are strong and do not need assistance or accolades from others, do we? We do not want to feel exposed. Recognize that experiencing resistance and finding the workout tough is normal.

Accepting compliments might be a strong measure of your self-esteem. Accept praises and allow yourself to experience vulnerability. Accepting that you are deserving of praises can assist you in increasing your self-esteem.

Exercise 2 – The game of appreciation

The objective of this game is to teach you to appreciate aspects of yourself that you previously overlooked (or like). It will work best if you have a regular partner with whom you can play the game. Tell your spouse three characteristics you like about them and invite them to do the same. Be as detailed as possible and don't be concerned with coming up with grandiose ideas. The following are some examples:

- ✓ I appreciate you preparing breakfast this morning despite your haste.
- ✓ I appreciate your picking up the children today.

✓   I appreciate how attentive you are to my concerns after work.

To continue:

Self-esteem is a nuanced subject. It is prevalent and often misinterpreted. It takes time and effort to overcome poor self-esteem. If you often feel unworthy, I recommend you to consult the following literature. If you discover that you have serious and persistent self-esteem difficulties as a result of reading these books, you may choose to visit a professional.

Nathaniel Branden's PhD book, The Six Pillars of Self-Esteem. Marilyn Sorensen, PhD, author of Breaking the Chain of Low Self-Esteem. Low Self-Esteem: Misunderstood and Misdiagnosed: Why You May Be Unable to Get the Help You Need, by Marilyn Sorensen, PhD.

The following is a concise synopsis of few of the major themes in each book:

Nathaniel Branden defined six self-esteem practices (or pillars) in his book, The Six Pillars of Self-Esteem; that you may work on to achieve a healthy self-esteem:

1. Living consciously: According to Nathaniel Branden, "living consciously" implies "striving to be aware of everything that influences our actions, purposes, worth, and goals—to the best of our ability, whatever that capacity may be—and acting in line with what we see and know."

2. Self-acceptance involves valuing yourself, treating yourself with respect, and asserting your right to exist. Self-acceptance serves as the foundation for developing self-esteem.

3. Self-responsibility: Recognizes that no one is coming to save you and that you are ultimately accountable for your own life. It is acknowledging your accountability for your decisions and actions. You are accountable for your time management and happiness. Because only you have the power to alter the course of your life.

4. Self-assertiveness: This refers to the act of recognizing one's desires, needs, and values and pursuing suitable forms of expression in reality.

5. Purposeful living: Is using your abilities to accomplish the objectives you have chosen. In other words, it refers to your capacity for setting and achieving objectives in all aspects of your life.

6. Personal integrity is defined as acting in accordance with one's principles, opinions, and ideas. It's when you can look in the mirror and be certain that you're doing the correct thing.

Marilyn Sorensen offers an excellent description of what self-esteem is and how it works in Breaking the Chain of Low Self-Esteem. Low self-esteem, the author adds, arises from your unfavorable image of yourself—a perspective that is primarily, if not totally, based on your negative interpretations of previous events. Fear and anxiety are a result of this erroneous perspective of reality. Your familial situation may have been a significant factor. Perhaps your parents had continually criticized you, leaving you with the impression that nothing you accomplished was ever good enough.

You may suddenly be convinced that you are less deserving than others. As a consequence, everything is filtered through this negative view of oneself. It's as if you're seeing reality through tinted glasses that filter out praise and praises and focus only on critiques.

The examples in her books will assist you in comprehending how low self-esteem manifests in everyday life. Additionally, Ms

Sorensen includes hundreds of practical activities that will assist you in being more conscious of your self-esteem difficulties and provide you with the skills necessary to achieve a more healthy self-esteem.

Defensive Thoughts

Are you continually justifying your actions? Are you outraged if someone makes an insult or disrespectful remark about you?

You get protective for very particular reasons. By being aware of these factors, you will have a greater understanding of yourself and will be able to let go of the impulse to protect oneself. To begin, let us examine why you get defensive.

Why do you get defensive?

The drive to safeguard your tale motivates you to defend yourself (or your ego). You are triggered and feel the need to protect your ego whenever it is attacked. There are, in my opinion, three primary reasons why you are triggered.

1. A portion of what you were told is true.

2. You think that some of what you were taught is true.

3. A fundamental belief of yours has been assailed.

Take note that while everyone's story is unique, what triggers you may not trigger someone else.

1. A portion of what you were told is true

Someone said something honest about you, and it stings. For example, he or she can accuse you of delaying on a certain task. You become defensive as a result of your reluctance to accept that fact. When that subject is brought up, emotional responses such as rage, denial, or self-criticism occur.

2. You think that some of what you were taught is true

You were taught something that you think is real and are now in pain. In this scenario, the complaints leveled against you may be unjustified. Nonetheless, you continue to experience pain. Why is this case? That is because the information you received validates the disempowering ideas you have about yourself. For instance, suppose you feel you are unworthy. This conviction motivates you to strive harder than everyone else. Now consider how you would feel if someone accused you of being slothful. Wouldn't you be offended? However, this would not be due to your true laziness, but to your conviction that you should work more.

3. A fundamental belief of yours has been assailed

Someone assaults one of your fundamental values directly or indirectly, and you feel compelled to defend yourself. This might be a religious conviction, a political conviction, or a more broad conviction about the world or oneself. The more ingrained this concept is in you, the more powerful your emotional response will be. Here is an excellent illustration:

Due to their belief that Donald Trump was wicked, numerous Liberals had significant emotional responses upon his election as president. Several individuals screamed and even grew violent. On the other hand, a sizable number of Conservatives applauded Trump's triumph.

How is it possible for individuals to respond so differently to the same event? This is due to their fundamental beliefs. Democrats and Republicans both take a firm stand for their political convictions. This resulted in outpourings of grief from hardline Democrats and joy from hardline Republicans.

When a firmly held belief is attacked or questioned, an emotional response occurs. The more ingrained the concept, the more powerful the emotional response when it is assailed. Someone who is willing to murder anybody who dares to question his or her faith is an extreme example.

How to make the most of this feeling in order to develop

Consider the circumstances that cause you distress. Whenever you are insulted, consider why. What conviction compelled you to defend yourself? Are you capable of letting go of this belief? And is this view based on fact?

This will teach you a great lot about yourself. You'll be able to let go of ideas that no longer serve you, and you'll understand that you seldom need to defend yourself.

ANXIETY AND CONFLICT

You may be wondering, "What is stress, and why do I get it?"

A lot of individuals feel that a scenario might be tense. To put it another way, there is no such thing as a circumstance that is stressful in and of itself. But I'm sure you deal with stress on a daily basis. And possibly more often than you'd want.

Tens of thousands of people die each year as a result of stress. Grieving the death of a loved one may do more damage than many illnesses and leave many families devastated. If you don't do something about your stress, it will become worse.

Taking charge of your own stress

As a result, you must take responsibility for your own stress. Because the more you accept responsibility for it, the less likely it is that you'll have it.

Stress occurs for a variety of causes and in a variety of contexts. A long commute, a stressful business meeting, or a disagreement with your spouse is all examples of things that might cause stress. Stress may be reduced in two ways:

- ✓ In order to prevent stressful circumstances and to improve your ability to handle difficult events.
- ✓ Learn how to lessen your stress levels with the help of these techniques.

How to utilize stress to your advantage

Make a list of the things that cause you the most stress.

Let's take a closer look at some of the things that cause you anxiety. Write down in the workbook what stresses you out the most throughout a regular week. Ten ideas are a good starting point.

Emotions are triggered by the way you perceive the world around you. The fact that you feel tension (or any other feeling) indicates that you've made up your mind about what's going on. You wouldn't have to worry about anything else.

Take a moment to review your list of stressful events. The following questions should be asked of oneself in each situation:

- ✓ Is it a difficult scenario to be in?
- ✓ What do I have to believe in order to feel stressed out in that particular situation?
- ✓ Specifically, what would I need to think in order to alleviate or eliminate the tension in that situation?

A traffic bottleneck may be frustrating, so let's pretend you're caught in one.

Is it a difficult scenario to be in? Definitely not. There is a traffic congestion, but nothing is wrong with it.

- Specifically, what do I need to think in order to feel stressed out in that particular circumstance?

I'd have to believe that:

Traffic jams are a sign that something is amiss in the transportation system.

In and of itself, the traffic gridlock is a stressful situation.

Instead of being caught in traffic, I should be on my way to where I need to be. I have the ability to take action.

- When faced with a stressful scenario, what beliefs might help me cope better?

In order for me to accept:

A traffic congestion is just another day in the life of a driver.

Even if I'm caught in traffic, I don't have to worry about it.

In the meanwhile, I'm stuck in a traffic congestion, and I don't need to get there where I'm going.

I'm unable to change it, so why not enjoy it or at least not worry about it.

Being able to cope with anxiety

Unlike stress, which is a reaction to something you are experiencing right now, worry is a reaction to something you are worried will happen in the future or something that happened in the past. When confronted with a difficult circumstance in the here and now, you feel the effects of stress.

Being stopped in traffic or having your boss shout at you are examples of stressful situations. Recalling (the past) or worrying pre-visualizing these frightening events (future). Your fears are unwarranted because of the following reasons:

There's nothing you can do about what's already occurred, and you have no influence over what could happen in the future.

Make a list of your anxieties as a kind of exercise.

Write down anything you're afraid of (past or future). Things you wrote in the last exercise may be relevant here. You may be concerned about the following:

- ✓ In terms of your own well-being
- ✓ What is the state of your finances? Your efforts are appreciated.
- ✓ Your personal connections, such as friendships and family ties.

Now, jot down at least 10 items you worry about on a regular basis.

Getting your mind at ease

As a consequence of constantly worrying about things that you can't control, you end up feeling anxious all the time. Make your life more difficult by doing so. Worries are a necessary part of managing stress and overcoming long-term anxieties. The best approach to achieve this is to make a distinction between what you can control and what you can't. You may categorize your concerns into three groups:

Things you can control, things you can influence, and things you can't influence at all.

Things you can influence, such as your own actions and behaviors, fall under this category. As an example, you may decide what to say and how to express it. You have the power to direct your own course of action in pursuit of your objectives.

Things you have some influence over, such as a job interview or a competition, are examples of this. It's impossible to guarantee victory in a tennis match, but you may influence the result to some extent. For example, you can work out more or employ a good coach. In the same way, you may prepare for a job interview by completing comprehensive research about the firm you are applying to or by doing a mock interview. However, you don't have complete influence over the interview's result.

It's unfortunate, because you have no influence over a large number of factors. Things like the weather, the economy, and traffic congestion are all examples of this.

Workout - Organize your thoughts

Take a look at your own list of stressful events. You may add C (control) or SC (some control) next to each item (No control). As soon as you begin to organize your thoughts, you begin to lessen your stress levels. Identifying the things in your life that you have no control over can help alleviate your anxiety.

Now, write down what you can do about the areas that you have some influence over. To relieve them, what concrete measures might you take?

Is it possible for you to let go of your need to control things that are out of your control?

Taking full responsibility for your anxiety and stressors

There is more to worry about than you realize. Ask yourself, "What would I do if I had complete control over these situations?" What may it look like in real life? Is there any way I can prevent this from happening?"

Often, you'll come to recognize that you have some degree of influence over these events. Changing, reframing, or removing them from your life is one way to do this.

Assume that traffic congestion are something you can't do anything about. This seems to be the case. Once you're stuck in traffic, there's nothing you can do. But, could you do things a little differently? ' What if you left sooner or took a different route?

Rethinking the scenario could be a good idea. Avoiding the problem emotionally by making traffic jams an enjoyable part of your day is one option. In this case it would be best to use your time by listening to audiobooks. Every day for a year, imagine how much you might learn just listening to audiobooks.

Things you can't control are on your list, so focus on them. Think of ways to alter, reinterpret, or completely remove these occurrences from your life.

Being mindful of what others think of you

Do you have a lot of insecurities? Let me explain why you worry so much about what other people think of you and what you can do to relieve the problem in this part.

In the grand scheme of things, you are the most important person on the planet.

When you recognize this, all else will fall into place. Try to recall a moment when you were in excruciating discomfort if you don't trust me. You might have a toothache, be recovering from surgery, or even have a broken limb from an accident. What were your thoughts at the time? Afraid you'd miss anything important because of the famine? Did you have any concerns about the deaths of innocents in the Middle East's wars?

No.

Pain was the only thing keeping you awake at night. Because you are the most important person on the planet, you deserve the best treatment. It's fair to worry about your emotional and physical health since you spend so much time by yourself.

Everyone on the globe is going through the same thing. As far as I'm concerned, I'm more important than you. Your friends, family, and coworkers, on the other hand, see it the same way.

Because you're always thinking about yourself, you tend to overestimate how frequently other people are thinking about you. People don't really give a damn about you. It's truly freeing, despite the fact that it sounds dismal. As a result, you no longer have to be self-conscious about your appearance.

A well-known axiom states:

There are three stages of maturity: the twenty-year-old stage, the forty-year-old stage (the point at which you stop caring what other people think), and the sixty-year-old stage.

Nobody else is keeping note of your blunders and missteps. People are merely preoccupied with their own concerns. In a nutshell, the general public does not:

- ✓ Keep a record of the times you've failed in the past.
- ✓ Take a close look at anything you put out there on the internet. Keep an eye out for your embarrassing moments.
- ✓ I frequently think of you, or
- ✓ Take as much interest in you as you do in yourself.
- ✓ You won't be loved by everyone.

To get their approval, you care what others think of you. You're under the impression that the ideal strategy is to keep a low profile. If this is the case, you may spend the rest of your life attempting to be the ideal person in order to get someone's affection.

However, this seldom happens. Whatever your accomplishments, there will always be individuals who don't like you. You may make an effort to improve the perception of yourself that others have of you, but none of those options will work. Because of their own values and views, people will perceive you the way they want to see you.

The approval of others will always be at the mercy of someone who bases their self-worth on what others think of them. What would happen if they suddenly decided they didn't like the way you were acting? Lack of self-approval can never be remedied by praise from others.

Trying too hard to please everyone puts you at danger of leading a life that is devoid of the freedom to be yourself. As a result, you'll wind up imitating your pals and satisfying everyone else except yourself, and that's a mistake.

It's none of your business what other people think of you.

You have no control over what other people think. In reality, it doesn't matter what other people think of you. It's your responsibility to convey your unique personality in the most genuine manner possible while maintaining the highest level of sincerity. In a nutshell, your job is to be the best version of yourself possible. After then, it's up to others whether or not they like you. Millions of people despise the most powerful individuals in the world, such as presidents and politicians.

As a result, refrain from making it your personal goal to alter how others see you. There is nothing wrong with people disliking you; everyone has the right to their own opinions. They have the right to apply their own interpretations to your actions and demeanor. Accepting that you don't have to be liked by everyone and that you can finally be yourself is an important part of your personal progress.

How to make the most of this feeling in order to progress

Having a lot of self-consciousness implies:

- ✓ Your self-image is important to you, and you have a mistaken perception of how others see you.
- ✓ You must address these two issues in order to quit being so self-conscious.

Begin by altering your perception of how others see you.

To stop worrying about what other people think of you, you must change the way you relate to others. To do this, you must acknowledge:

People don't pay attention to you, and you don't pay attention to them.

Workout No. 1: Acknowledging that Nobody Gives A F*ck

You'll have a deeper appreciation for how little others care about you if you go through this exercise.

Pick someone you're familiar with. It might be a close friend, a new acquaintance, or even a coworker.

Consider how frequently you think about that individual on a regular basis.

Assume that person's position now. How often do you think about him or her on a daily basis? Does he or she pay attention to everything you do or say? What do you suppose he or she is pondering at the moment?

At the very least, have two additional persons participate in this process.

While doing this task, you'll likely come to understand that others are just too busy to think about you very frequently. After all, they spend their days and nights alone. There is no one more important to them than themselves. That's not the case with you. And it's only natural that this should happen, as well.

Realizing that you don't give a fuck about what others think

Nobody cares that much about your feelings. What follows will help you see this.

As you go about your day, try to recall the names and faces of everyone you come into contact with. The waitress or other patrons at the restaurant where you had lunch, passersby on the street, and so on and so forth are all possible candidates.

Take a moment to reflect on how much you have previously thought about each of these persons. Most likely, you didn't even consider them.

Clearly, you don't have the luxury of worrying about the opinions of others. The majority of the time, you're simply thinking about your own interests. To suggest you lack empathy or are a selfish person is not to imply you lack compassion or are a selfish jerk. Basically, you're just being human.

Stop obsessing on your own perception of yourself.

It's likely that you're extremely self-conscious since you're preoccupied with how others view you. You may be seeking their favor or fearing that they may be critical of you. Getting rid of this self-image is critical.

Self-image may be released via physical exercise.

Make a list of the things you're scared of being criticized for: As a result, maybe you're apprehensive about your appearance or fearful of making a mistake.

Make a list of the reasons why you're invested: What's the deal with this? Are you concerned about the image you're attempting to protect? Do you worry that you won't be able to live up to the picture that others have of you? Are you worried that you'll be rejected if you say or do anything incorrectly?

To assist you deal with the things you're worried about, you should do this activity now. The exercises suggested in the section 'Letting go of your emotions' should also be completed.

Finally, keep in mind that your words and actions will always be interpreted by others according to their own values and beliefs. In order to show off your individuality, you must allow others to view you as they see fit.

Resentment

When you resent someone, you are enraged at them for failing to act the way you desired. Perhaps they betrayed their commitments, or perhaps they fell short of your expectations. Perhaps you thought they owed you anything but failed to fulfill their obligation?

Resentment often grows when you are unable to communicate successfully with someone you despise. That is, when you did not share your feelings of pain or when you did not articulate your needs and desires, believing they would naturally be met. It may also develop when you express your emotions but are unable to let them go and forgive. "Resentment is like swallowing poison and hoping it kills your enemies," Nelson Mandela reportedly stated. It just does not work.

People who are resentful

As is the case with every other emotion, resentment intensifies according to the formula: interpretation + identification + repetition = intense feelings.

You may harbor animosity against someone for years over a very small occurrence if you:

Your assessment of the occurrence

Your identification with the narrative you're giving yourself about it, and/or the amount of times you mentally repeat the experience.

As an example, suppose one of your pals 'betrayed you' by declining to invite you to a party. In your opinion, your buddy has actually betrayed you, and you hold a grudge against him. You can't help yourself from wondering, "How could he have done that to me?" For weeks, the notion grips you, and you resolve to break all relations with him. You're still resentful of him months afterwards. Take note that the experience is not distressing in and of itself. What generates animosity is how you perceive an incident.

Is it conceivable, now, that your interpretation was incorrect? What if your buddy felt you would be uninterested in attending the party? What if he believed you were too preoccupied? True, he should have welcomed you at the very least, but nobody is perfect. If you'd set your perception aside and challenged him at the moment, maybe the outcome would have been different.

The danger of allowing bitterness to fester

Often, your hesitation or unwillingness to address the individuals you despise adds fuel to the fire. Rather than that, you keep replaying in your mind what (you believe) occurred. As a consequence, your animosity intensifies over time. This is particularly true if you deal with individuals you despise on a daily basis.

How to develop through resentment

When you are unable to forgive and go on with your life, resentment develops. It is the effect of being fixated on the past rather than on what may be in the future. When you are confronted with resentment, you are given the chance to practice forgiving and letting go, and, more significantly, to learn to love yourself.

Resentment is here to remind you that you must appreciate yourself and place a premium on your mental health. Your mental health must take precedence above being right, exacting retribution, or disliking someone else. In a nutshell, going past anger is making a proclamation of love to oneself in order to move forward, while also demonstrating compassion toward others.

Self-love

To paraphrase Nelson Mandela, bitterness is a poison you willingly drank. Resentment is the weed in your garden that you let to flourish. When you feel anger, you think that something to which you were lawfully entitled was stolen from you unfairly. It might be someone else's trust, respect, or affection, for example. As a consequence, you may feel as if you have been personally assaulted.

Resentment will persist as long as your want to be right and avenge yourself outweighs your desire for peace of mind. It will continue to develop as long as you continue to feed the feeling with resentment-filled thoughts. And it will continue to exist as long as you suppress it. That is why it is critical that you prioritize your mental health and learn to forgive others as well as yourself.

Others' love

Your capacity for anger release is proportional to your amount of compassion. Compassion makes it simpler to let go of animosity. One critical point to remember is that individuals always behave according to their degree of awareness (or unconsciousness). While you may wish someone had behaved differently toward you, the likelihood is that he or she was unable to do so.

Thus, rather of referring to individuals as either good or evil, it is more correct to refer to them as aware or unconscious. When people commit atrocities against you, it is often due to their lack of awareness or a poor emotional state at the moment.

Regrettably, the majority of individuals are highly conditioned. Their upbringing shapes their behavior. Individuals often behave in the same manner as their parents, which is why you frequently read about individuals who have been mistreated by their parents being abusive toward their children.

According to Eckhart Tolle's The Power of Now:

Because the mind is conditioned by the past, it is always seeking to recreate what it knows and is acquainted with. Even if it is uncomfortable, it is at least familiar. The mind is usually drawn to the familiar. The unknown is perilous because it is uncontrollable. That is why the mind is opposed to and dismissive of the present moment.

In summary, the (unconscious) human mind's inclination is to adhere to and replicate past patterns. If you examine your family history, you're likely to see certain trends. You will see how individuals are socially conditioned. This demonstrates how difficult it is for individuals to break apart from established habits.

I used to be resentful of my mother's over protectiveness. I blamed her for not encouraging me to develop, yet her actions only served to make me weaker. Perhaps this was one of the motivating factors for me to go on a personal development path. However, I recognized she was not malicious. She acted in good faith and did the best she could.

The idea is that individuals do the best they can with what they have, given who they are and how much conditioning they have received. They, too, make several errors. Every single one of us does. It is a natural element of being human.

One of the most absurd things we as humans attempt is to alter the past. What occurred in the past was intended to occur. Because it occurred. Now the issue is, what are your plans in response?

How to overcome resentment

To begin letting go of resentment, we'll address the significance of the following:

1. Modification/re-evaluation of your interpretation

2. Confronting the circumstance

3. Forgiveness (emancipation from identification), and

4. Forgetfulness (stopping the repetition).

Resentment arises as a consequence of your perception of an event that occurred to you. This interpretation induces feelings of betrayal and wrath, as well as a desire for vengeance. By replaying the scenario in your mind, you enable anger to develop and, since you avoid facing the event or person causing your resentment, the feeling continues to grow.

To avoid developing resentment, you must rethink your view of what occurred when confronted with the scenario or person you despise. After that, you must be prepared to forgive and let go of your anger. Finally, you must make the decision to forget. This requires refraining from rehearsing the scenario in your head incessantly.

1. Modification/re-evaluation of your interpretation

To put things in perspective, it's critical that you examine your understanding of what occurred. Perhaps you exaggerated the situation? Is it conceivable that you perceived anything incorrectly? Consider what occurred precisely. Once your interpretation is eliminated, just the harsh facts remain. By examining what really occurred, you may get useful insights and be able to replace your present perspective with a more empowered one.

2. Confronting the circumstance

If your animosity is focused towards certain persons, you may choose to have an open dialogue with them and express your feelings.

Often, resentment develops as a result of your failure to communicate your sentiments to the person you dislike. This is often motivated by fear: fear of seeming vulnerable, fear of causing harm to the other person, or fear of badly influencing your connection with that person. If you are unable to speak directly with that individual, an

As an alternative, you may write a letter. Even if you decide not to send the letter, the process of composing it may help you release some of your animosity.

3. Forgiving

Now that you've discovered a means of expressing yourself, you may begin to forgive. You've weighed the evidence and reconsidered your interpretation. You had an honest dialogue with the person you resent, if necessary. You've accomplished what needed to be accomplished and may now let go.

Consider the harmful repercussions of resentment. Make a note of how it impacts your happiness and mental well-being. Bear in mind that resentment is a byproduct of your connection to the past. Forgiveness is just reconnecting with what is true, the present, while letting go of what is false, the past. After that, release it. Consider how your life would be different and how you would feel if you were free of resentment. Do it immediately. Then release. Forgive.

Bear in mind that forgiveness is an act of self-love. You forgive not only out of kindness, but because your happiness is more important than anything else. As you forgive, you release your connection to your narrative and disassociate yourself from the associated ideas. To release resentment, use the five-step procedure described in the section 'Letting go of your emotions.'

4. Forgetting

Finally, let go. Forgetting occurs when you cease to entertain resentful thoughts and just go on. Allow such ideas to pass. They will eventually lose their strength.

Jealousy

When you are envious, you want for something that someone else has but you do not. We all experience jealousy on sometimes, and this is not anything you should blame on yourself. I'll explain how jealousy operates and provide some remedies in this part.

How to utilize envy to your advantage

Jealousy is a reaction to the notion that you are not good enough. It is motivated by a sense of deprivation and shortage. You want something that someone else has, assuming that it would satisfy you. Alternatively, you are fearful of losing something or someone you consider to be yours.

Jealousy might assist you in identifying what you really want.

Jealousy may alert you to the fact that you're on the incorrect track and can assist you in determining what you really want. For instance, Susan Cain noted in her book Quiet that she often felt envious of her acquaintances who were authors or psychiatrists. Interestingly, despite the fact that she was a lawyer at the time, she was not envious of successful attorneys, as many of her legal colleagues were. This brought her to the realization that she was not destined to be a lawyer. As a consequence, she decided to pursue a profession as a writer.

I experienced a like encounter. While I was a consultant, I had no jealousy for or admiration for the successful individuals in my organization. On the other side, I felt jealous of successful personal development bloggers and YouTubers along my personal development path. I was especially envious of two such individuals when I learned they were accomplishing just what I want. I envisioned how amazing it would be to assist others and contribute to society while still learning and improving. This is why I began writing a blog and began publishing books. As you can see, envy may be helpful when utilized appropriately.

Exercise - Identify someone about whom you are envious.

Make a list of those you are envious of. Now, what does this say about you and your life goals?

Jealousy may indicate a scarcity mentality.

In other instances, envy may suggest that you are working from a scarcity perspective. Allow me to illustrate this further with an example from my own life. When I see bestselling authors, I sometimes feel envy. I feel as if they are robbing me of my piece of the pie, and I am just as deserving of success as they are. I'm not proud of this sensation, but I also don't blame myself for it.

This sense of envy originates from the assumption that there is a finite quantity of success accessible. Thus, each time someone achieves a little degree of success, they are taking a piece of the action from you. Surprisingly, this is often not the case. If anything, the reverse is true for authors. The more a writer collaborates with other authors, the higher his or her prospects of success are. A writer who attempts to accomplish everything on their own is almost certain to fail. Of course, this is not confined to authors. By transforming your perspective from one of competition to one of collaboration, you may transition from a state of scarcity to one of plenty.

Nowadays, when I see other authors succeed, I am reminded of what wonderful news this is. After all, if they can accomplish it, then surely I can as well. And the more successful my other authors become, the more capable they are of assisting me in the future. This also works in reverse. The more I assist others,

The more successful authors are, the more they will be able to assist me in the future. As Zig Ziglar put it, "You can have whatever you want in life if you simply help other people obtain it." Bear in mind that whatever that other individuals can accomplish, you can do as well. Additionally, keep in mind that success is not a finite resource.

Consider a period in the past when you were envious of another person's success. Now inquire as to why you felt that way. Then consider the following:

- ✓ What would it be like to assist the individual?
- ✓ How am I to collaborate with this individual?
- ✓ Why is that individual's achievement beneficial to me?

Jealousy may indicate that you need to work on your self-esteem.

Perhaps you're concerned that your boyfriend or girlfriend will cheat on you or leave you for another. This is often motivated by the feeling that you are not good enough on your own and that you want your partner or girlfriend to 'complete' you. Regrettably (or luckily), just as you have no influence over what others think of you or how they act, you also have no control over your loved one's thoughts or conduct. Often, the urge to dominate your spouse is precisely what drives them away. While being envious on occasion is natural, if you are extremely jealous, it is critical that you examine inside. Your uncertainties and concerns are often the result of low self-esteem and the feeling that you cannot or will not be loved.

Jealousy may manifest itself in the following ways:

Attempting to exert control over your partner:

- You may monitor their phone or emails or restrict them from seeing their friends.
- You may expect your spouse to act a particular way, and when he or she does not, you may feel deceived. This arises from the conviction that You should not be required to communicate your desires or needs to your spouse. He or she should be able to make an educated estimate.

Imagining what isn't there: By extrapolating facts, you create an infinite number of tales in your imagination.

I urge you to go to the part under 'Not being good enough' to learn how to cultivate a stronger sense of self-worth.

Jealousy often arises as a consequence of comparison with others. It is critical to recognize that this form of comparison is often as ineffective as it is prejudiced. Indeed, apples to apples comparisons are uncommon. You see some of your friends' accomplishments but fail to recognize that this is just a portion of the whole. While they may seem to be happy and successful on the surface, they may be dissatisfied or even depressed. The argument is that rather than presuming your pals are happier than you, it is more prudent to believe you are equally pleased.

Additionally, avoid focusing only on areas where your peers seem to have it better than you. Perhaps you concentrate on their higher income or the fact that they have a spouse while you are alone. Alternatively, you may be envious of their inherent qualities and skills. The issue here is that you do not do a 'apple to apple' comparison. You minimize your own abilities or characteristics that make you feel inferior to others.

Even worse, you may often find yourself comparing yourself to various other individuals. You examine the areas in which they excel and then compare your own life to theirs. Naturally, not very well. How could you possibly compete against the combined strength of multiple individuals! Can you see how skewed and implausible this comparison is? Nonetheless, many of us do this unknowingly.

The basic conclusion is that if you experience jealousy, it may be due to this form of unfair comparison. Rather than that, why not compare your 'today' self to your 'yesterday' self? After all, all you can do is strive to be a better version of yourself than you were yesterday, last month, or last year. Due to the fact that every one of us begins with unique circumstances, abilities, and personalities, there is no such thing as a fair comparison.

Comparing apples to apples

This practice will assist you in making more accurate comparisons to others.

Choose someone with whom you often compare yourself. Make a list of all the things you do better than that individual.

DEPRESSION

For those who have lost all hope of ever achieving their dreams and are unable to accept their current situation, there is non-clinical depression. After a sad occurrence in your life, or more gradually when various areas of your life begin to fall apart, you may begin to suffer from depression. Depression is caused by a sense of hopelessness in one or more aspects of your life. Here are a few examples:

Jobless, you have little possibility of finding a new one to meet your standards.

You're unwell and don't expect to get better any time soon.

You and your ex-partner got divorced, so you only get to visit your kids every now and again.

The odds are stacked against you in your search for love.

It feels like you'll never get out of debt since you're in so much of it.

You lost a loved one.

Depression may also be caused by more "everyday", less severe circumstances, such as the ones listed above. Some individuals may get sad as a result of obsessively reflecting on the past or worrying about the future. This might happen even if they haven't experienced anything noteworthy in their life.

You must remember that depression, like other emotional states, is neither good nor bad; it just is. Depression is not who you are. All things being equal, you existed before, during, and after the event.

Anxiety is an ongoing process.

Even while it may seem as if you are suffering from depression, it is really a result of the negative ideas you identify with. Because of this, you bear part of the blame for your sadness. When someone is sad, does it indicate that they should feel guilty or shame themselves? Not at all! Never. However, you shouldn't worry about your feelings at all. That would be a waste of my time. In reality, what it implies is that you have the potential to change your present emotional state since you contributed to its creation. That's fantastic, isn't it?

Remember Dr. David K. Reynolds' first-hand experience with depression? He wrote the following:

Depression can be created by sitting slouched in a chair, shoulders hunched, head hanging down. Repeat these words over and over: 'There's nothing anybody can do. No one can help. It's hopeless. I'm helpless. I give up.' Shake your head, sigh, cry. In general, act depressed and the genuine feeling will follow in time.

— DAVID K. REYNOLDS, CONSTRUCTIVE LIVING.

One can only blame oneself for the depth of David K. Reynolds' despair. It was a conscious effort on my part to adopt particular body language, say certain phrases, and think certain thoughts in order to achieve this result. To get depressed, he had to do a certain set of actions.

Because you have the ability to 'make' despair, you also have the ability to escape it, which is encouraging news. Disregarding negative ideas and replacing them with more upbeat ones might be difficult when one is suffering from depression. Though you may believe good feelings like thankfulness, pleasure, or happiness at first appear to have no effect, they will eventually become more powerful.

However, you may also feel other unpleasant feelings, including wrath. At first, you may choose to dismiss your feelings of rage. Doing so may be encouraged by your loved ones, who don't want to see you furious. Even while rage may be debilitating, it can also be a stepping stone to better mental health and recovery from depression. Make sure to keep in mind that any feeling other than despair may assist and learn to accept whatever emotional state appears to offer you more energy, and therefore more strength to advance up the emotional ladder."

David K. Reynolds also believes that sentiments may change with time, even in persons who are sad. According to him, "There are ripples and waves of milder feelings in the darkest sadness." When you're feeling a little better, you may take advantage of those moments to do whatever it is that will benefit you at the time.

How to get the most out of sadness for personal growth

Depression is an indication that you've lost your sense of perspective and perspective. Aren't we one of the only creatures on the planet capable of suffering from depression? In order to become lost in their thoughts and get imprisoned by demoralizing tales, they are the only ones capable of doing it.

The presence of depression is a warning that you need to disconnect from your thoughts and re-establish your connection with the current moment. A compelling call to let go of the identity you've held onto for so long. Because of this, you've come to think that you should be doing what you're doing.

particular things, like as achieving a certain financial goal, changing one's way of life, or rising in the social hierarchy.

Depression forces you to re-establish contact with your physical self and your feelings, as well as to let go of your thoughts. After all, isn't it true that your thoughts are what caused the sadness to begin with? To avoid thinking, those who are suffering from a great deal of loss, sadness, or melancholy may choose to keep themselves occupied. More pondering seldom helps when you're sad. When it comes to depression, you don't see many individuals utilizing their brains to get out of it.

In other words, you want to be back in touch with your physical self instead of just thinking about it. It has been established that regular exercise is a fantastic strategy to lift your spirits and has shown to be helpful in this regard. Refer to the section "Exercise Benefits" for further details.

A severe case of depression may cause individuals to become disconnected from their thoughts. When this occurs, the credibility of their narrative is immediately shattered. In his book, The Power of Now, Eckhart Tolle recounts how this occurred to him. He was awakened by a startling waking, and his thoughts were paralyzed. Here is what he had to say about it:

This withdrawal must have been so complete that this false, suffering self immediately collapsed, just as if a plug had been pulled out of an inflatable toy.

— ECKHART TOllE

To summarize, sadness instructs you to let go of your ego and reestablish contact with the actual world. It encourages you to live more in the present moment by getting you out of your head, which is only capable of remembering the past or speculating about the future. In the case of severe depression, a medical expert should be consulted; however here are some self-help tactics for depression that may be used in the interim:

Exercise enables you to reacquaint yourself with your physical and emotional self.

You must get out of your head if you want to recover from depression. Depression is easier to get out of if you 'feel' your way out rather than 'think' your way out.

I'd dare to estimate that for the majority of individuals; more than 90% of their time is spent thinking. They only experience brief periods of clarity when they are completely awake and fully aware of their surroundings. For example, they don't pay attention to what others have to say, but:

Listen to what they have to say and make your own judgments based on it.

Consider what they're going to say next or get absorbed in their ideas.

All of these occurrences occur on a 'mind' level and demonstrate how humans are not present in their entirety. Negative emotions are felt by people who either dwell in the past or the future (i.e., in their minds). Getting in touch with your physical and emotional self might be as simple as the following:

Exercise: Exercising may help you relax your mind and reconnect with your body while also improving your mood, as we've previously described.

Meditation may help you become more aware of your ideas and less attached to them. Instead of being lost in your thoughts, feelings, and sensations, meditation serves as a tool to help you reconnect with reality.

Activity: You can prevent overthinking if you keep your mind occupied. Keep your mind off of your sadness by focusing on anything else instead of thinking constantly about it.

Look out for the welfare of others: Alfred Adler once told his melancholy patients, "You may be healed in fourteen days if you follow this prescription," according to Dale Carnegie's book How to Stop Worrying and Start Living. Every day, focus on how you can make someone else happy. Distracting your attention away from your own problems and onto the good things in life, whether or not they are true, is a certain way to alleviate stress.

Unfortunately, none of these activities will be appealing to you if you're depressed. While it may be difficult at first, once you get moving and keep yourself active, things will become easier and easier. As a result, it's critical to proceed cautiously and incrementally.

Afraid/ Discomfort

We face nervousness whenever we attempt anything new. We fear the unknown. This is why we want to stick to our everyday routines and our comfort zones. This makes perfect sense from our brain's perspective. If our existing habits keep us secure and protect us from possible threats to our existence (or the survival of our ego), why change them? This explains why humans often repeat the same routines or ideas. This is also why we may encounter significant internal opposition while attempting to change.

As a result, when we attempt to push ourselves beyond our comfort zones, we encounter dread and pain. Now, do we want to spend the majority of our life in the same location and avoid taking chances, or do we want to chase our ambitions and discover what we actually are capable of becoming? We must bear in mind that the majority of our anxieties are a danger to our ego, not to our existence. They are often not tangible dangers, but imagined ones. We risk losing out on life if we play it safe, and we may regret it later.

The following are some frequent anxieties that you may encounter:

Fear of rejection: You are fearful of rejection. This may take the form of physical rejection by a certain group, although it is often more subtle. For instance, you may be fearful of the following:

Making a statement that others may not approve of, or approaching someone and being rejected, or sharing your work and being chastised for it.

Fear of failure: You fear failure. This is often motivated by a profound fear of not being good enough, i.e. you dread mockery and feel that failure would undermine your self-esteem.

Human beings have a natural aversion to loss, which is why we are often more driven to avoid a loss than to acquire a gain.

You're terrified of upsetting others. Perhaps as a result of the notion that you are not significant enough. As a consequence, you may be hesitant to affirm yourself out of concern that you would look selfish.

You are terrified of success. You may be concerned that you will be unable to maintain it with the additional burden on your shoulders.

How to utilize fear to your advantage

Fear of doing anything new is often an indication that you should proceed nonetheless. This suggests an outstanding chance for personal development. Fear, like any other emotion, lives just in your imagination. This is why we often discover what a fool we were after completing something we were first hesitant to begin.

Individuals who achieve their most audacious ambitions often do so because they are ready to go beyond their comfort zone. They gradually develop an ability to tolerate the unpleasant. Consider one activity you were previously terrified to do but are now comfortable doing. For example, I'm sure you were terrified the first time you drove a vehicle or on your first day of work. Now, haven't you become used to it?

The fact is that humans possess an extraordinary capacity for learning. The trick is to get used to occasional pain. By avoiding confronting your concerns on a regular basis, you significantly restrict your growth potential. Staying inside your comfort zone may also destroy your sense of self-esteem, since you are aware that you are not doing what you should be doing.

In nature, there is a law: things either grow or die. The same is true for people. When individuals remain inside their comfort zone, they begin to die on the inside. Allow this not to happen to you. As Benjamin Franklin put it, "Some persons die at the age of twenty-five and are not buried until they reach the age of seventy-five." Ascertain that' some individuals' does not include you!

Taking the initiative

The first step in breaking out of your comfort zone is to acknowledge that even the most successful people on the planet experience dread. Courage is not a lack of dread; it is taking action in the face of fear. Courage is accepting that fear will not go away and doing with what you want to achieve nevertheless. There is no boldness without fear. By confronting fear on a consistent basis, you create bravery and make it a habit.

You do not have to ignore fear or become numb to it in order to act. Rather than that, you must embrace the truth that fear will not go away and learn to live with it. Then you must determine whether or not to act.

Exercise - Push yourself beyond your comfort zone

To begin breaking out of your comfort zone, ask yourself, "What is the one thing I should be doing but have been putting off due to fear?" Once you've accomplished that one task, you're likely to feel a feeling of accomplishment and aliveness. This is a good indication that you're on the correct route. Consider it a prize from your brain for venturing beyond your comfort zone.

Drag One's Feet

Procrastination is mostly a psychological problem. While there are some successful ways for overcoming procrastination, the majority of the time, learning to regulate your emotions effectively is the key to overcoming your proclivity for delayed action.

Why are you a procrastinator?

Individuals procrastinate for a variety of reasons. Several of them are listed below:

- ✓ The assignment is tedious.
- ✓ The work is deemed trivial.
- ✓ The job is really too difficult (or perceived as such) You're terrified of doing a terrible job, and/or you're a chronic slacker.

Consider if you would delay if the activity was enjoyable, viewed as critical, and so simple that you couldn't fail.

Fear, I think, is the primary motivator of procrastination. People will prefer put off a task if they are afraid they would perform a lousy job. While they may tell themselves that the work is not critical or urgent, or that they are exhausted, the reality is that they are afraid.

Keep in mind that procrastination is not an indication of laziness or that anything is wrong with you. Everybody procrastinates. However, if you procrastinate often, it may imply that you either lack self-esteem or lack self-discipline.

How to develop through procrastination

Procrastination may indicate that you place an excessive amount of trust in what your mind is telling you. Rather than being the ruler of your mind, you've ceded control to it. This is at the expense of: not living the life you want, not achieving your goals, and suffering from poor self-esteem, guilt, and sadness.

Bear in mind when your mind says, "You're exhausted." "Let's take a break," or "Let's do it tomorrow," are not commands. You are not obligated to follow it. You are not a product of your feelings. You, on the other hand, are not your thoughts. Whatever idea crosses your mind, you have the option of accepting it or ignoring it.

Now I'd like to offer a sixteen-step approach for overcoming procrastination with you. Not to worry; it's not quite as complex as it seems.

How to Eliminate Procrastination in 16 Easy Steps

1. Recognize the underlying causes of procrastination.

The first step is to identify the source of your procrastination. As previously established, there are distinct causes for procrastination. Typically, it involves fear, and the mind instructs you that the greatest approach to avoid dread is to do nothing. In other words, to delay. Another reason you put off completing a job is because it is tough. You want to minimize discomfort and enhance pleasure. This is the how your brain operates. Additionally, you may postpone due to a lack of motivation. This occurs when the job at hand is not connected to a larger goal that motivates you. If you're lacking motivation, consider why. Consider the following alternatives:

Assign the job Eliminate the assignment

Reframe your perception of the work to include it in a larger (and more interesting) picture.

Restructure the work to make it more manageable, and/or simply begin (see step 13).

Spend some time recognizing all of the factors that contribute to your procrastination. Be truthful to yourself.

2. Remind yourself of the expense associated with procrastination

Procrastination is not a trivial matter and has serious implications.

Procrastination's immediate result is that you will accomplish significantly less than you might throughout your time on earth.

Procrastination may have the unintended effect of making you feel horrible about yourself. You may blame yourself for failing to accomplish what you know you should be doing, eroding your self-esteem and generating unneeded anxiety.

Exercise - the price of inaction

Now, grab a piece of paper and jot down the expenses of procrastination.

- ✓ How does it effect your mental health?
- ✓ What is your self-esteem?
- ✓ Your capacity for achieving your goals?

The more frustrated you get with procrastination, the more inclined you are to take action.

3. Uncover your narrative

The third step in overcoming procrastination is to ascertain the reason for it. When you sense the need to postpone, what are you telling yourself? What thoughts occur to you? What justifications do you employ? Several frequent justifications include the following:

I'm too exhausted.

I'll do it tomorrow, and/or I'll do a lousy job. It is irrelevant.

Let us address a few of these justifications immediately.

I'm too exhausted

While this is true, you must understand that you are not your thoughts. You are not required to pay attention to your thinking. David Goggins, a Navy SEAL, employs the forty percent rule. This rule claims that even when you believe you're at your limit, you're only utilizing 40% of your brain's capability. The basic conclusion is that you have enormous reservoirs of energy that you may draw from when you are exhausted. As a result, spending two hours after work on your side company will not kill you.

I'm going to do a lousy job.

If you plan anything for today, it indicates that you feel you can do it. Thus, worry of performing a lousy job is irrelevant in this case. After all, if you believe you will do poorly today, what makes you believe you will perform better tomorrow? Most likely, you will not. That is only a narrative you are telling yourself.

I'll take care of it tomorrow.

Performing the task tomorrow may not be a huge issue. However, if you lack the discipline necessary to complete today's duties, how likely are you to construct your perfect life in the future? Remember, it is ultimately through self-discipline that you will be able to design your future existence. To accomplish anything worthwhile in life, time, effort, and self-discipline are necessary.

It is not critical.

Even if it is true, failing to complete a scheduled job produces an open loop. Then, somewhere in the back of your mind, you remember that you still have that duty to perform. If you continue to put off responsibilities, you will quickly lose motivation. At some time, you may even find yourself feeling trapped for no apparent reason.

Exercise - Jot down your justifications

Begin by being aware of all the justifications you make. Make a list of them and then address them one by one. They have authority over you because you have allowed them to. Make a commitment to resolving them.

4. Rewrite your narrative

Consider your justifications. Are you too exhausted? Are you pressed for time? Are you attempting to do things flawlessly? After identifying your narrative, build a new, more powerful one to replace your previous justifications. Consider the following examples:

I don't have time for that; anything I'm devoted to, I find and create time for.

I'm too exhausted, yet I have command of my head and more vitality than I suppose. When I schedule a task, I ensure that it is completed.

Then, surround your new tale with affirmations or mantras. Each morning and throughout the day, repeat them to yourself until they become ingrained in your identity. Bear in mind that procrastination is a habit. You want to retrain your mind and establish a new habit: the habit of completing assignments.

You schedule regardless of how you feel. (For further information, see the section 'Conditioning your mind.')

5. Defining your 'why'

Procrastination is often the result of a lack of motivation. When you're passionate about something, you don't flee from it, do you? No. You can't wait to get started!

Consider the chores that you often procrastinate on. Why is this the case? How can you include these chores into your vision to increase your motivation? Are you able to modify these tasks? Are you able to glean anything from these tasks? Can you see yourself experiencing a sense of accomplishment as you finish these tasks?

The more compelling your rationale, you're 'why,' the simpler it will be to overcome your procrastination propensity.

6. Identify the ways in which you divert your attention.

The next stage is to become aware of all the ways in which you divert your attention. How do you procrastinate on your own? Is it taking a stroll? Are you a YouTube viewer? Consuming coffee? Or maybe you could spend your time reading books on how to combat procrastination?

Unless you are conscious of every manifestation of procrastination in your life, you will have a difficult time conquering it.

Make a note of all the ways you procrastinate in this exercise.

Take a few moments to use the free worksheet to track all the ways you procrastinate.

7. Adhere to the impulse

As you are tempted to *insert your distraction here*, maintain your focus on the feeling. What are your feelings? Permit yourself to experience the feeling. Make no judgments about yourself. You are not to blame. Simply accept what exists. You will benefit as a result better control over your thoughts, (for further information, see the chapter on 'Letting go of your emotions.')

8. Keep track of everything you do

To gauge your productivity and get insight into how you procrastinate, keep a notepad of everything you accomplish. Do this for a week. Make a note of each time you transition from one task to another. Ensure that you record the amount of time you spend on each job.

By the end of the week, you'll have a better idea of how much time you spend on 'real' work and how much time you spend on self-distraction. Take caution; you may be stunned.

9. Always act with a clear purpose in mind

Before beginning a job, ensure that you understand precisely what has to be done. Consider the following: What am I attempting to achieve here? How will the final product look? This manner, you'll prevent your mind from concocting reasons.

10. Construct your surroundings

Your intellect despises difficulty. It desires simplicity. As such, ensure that any friction or impediment is removed so that you may begin working on your assignment immediately. Consider the following:

If you wish to run, have your running clothes next to your bed so you may go for a run immediately upon waking (after a full warm-up first, of course).

For computer-related activities, clear your desk of any distractions and ensure that you have fast access to all necessary files.

11. Begin modestly

Rather of placing yourself under a lot of strain, why not start small? Rather of writing two pages of your book, maybe one paragraph would enough. Why not begin with five minutes instead of an hour of exercise? Simplifying your chores will assist you in overcoming procrastination. Additionally, it will enable you to gain momentum. Therefore, wherever possible, begin modest to alleviate pressure.

12. Identify quick victories

Daily encounters with challenging activities can set you up for failure and sap your drive. Reduce the size of your projects and establish manageable goals. This will do the following:

Permit you to develop the habit of finishing all of your assignments completely.

As you accrue quick successes, your self-esteem will grow, and you will feel less compelled to postpone.

Every day, set little objectives and work toward them regularly for a few weeks. By doing so, you will boost your self-esteem and improve your ability to execute difficult activities in the future. Bear in mind that getting things done is a habit that, like any other, can be exercised and taught.

13. Simply begin

Oftentimes, after you begin working on a job, you will enter what is referred to as 'the flow,' in which everything seems easy. In some cases, you get so absorbed in your activity that motivation becomes irrelevant.

The quickest method to reach a 'flow state' is to begin. To simplify, commit to working on a job for five minutes and observe what occurs. Remove any pressure or desire to do well, and allow yourself to make a mistake. Frequently, you'll find yourself working on the assignment for far longer than anticipated than was initially intended. Keep in mind that the more attention-demanding the work, the more likely you are to enter the flow fast.

Additionally, you may use the 5-Second Rule, which Mel Robbins developed in her book, The 5 Second Rule. According to this guideline, you have a 5-second window in which to act before your mind talks you out of it. (For further information on the 5 Second Rule, see the section on 'Conditioning your thinking.')

14. Establish everyday practices that will benefit you

If you have a proclivity for procrastinating on crucial activities, make a commitment to begin working on them first thing in the morning. For instance, if you want to write a novel, begin each morning by writing. Begin small. For example, make a small goal of writing fifty words each day and commit to it each morning. Maintaining this plan can help you create a writing habit and reduce the likelihood of procrastinating.

15. Make use of visuals

Additionally, you may employ visualization to assist you in overcoming procrastination. The following are two particular approaches to do this:

1. Visualize yourself doing the task: Imagine turning on the computer, opening the file, and starting to write. Consider donning your running shoes and heading out for a run. This technique has been demonstrated to boost the probability that you will complete the assignment.

Experiment with it.

2. Visualize yourself completing the task: How would you feel after completing the task? Liberated? Happy? Proud? Now, imagine how you would feel if you had successfully finished your assignment. As a result, you'll notice an increase in motivation, which will inspire you to continue working on your assignment.

16. Promote accountability

If you're having difficulty finishing a task, you may need some responsibility. When I'm prone to procrastination, I prefer to send a message to a buddy informing him that I'm going to do a task by a particular date.

Another strategy to increase responsibility is to establish a regular communication channel with an accountability partner. You may meet with him or her once a week to discuss your objectives. Consider the critical activities you're likely to put off and assign each one a specified date. Then, once you finish a task, you may send an email to your accountability partner notifying him or her.

If you follow this sixteen-step approach, you should be able to conquer or greatly lessen your procrastination inclination.

Lack of Inspiration

Lack of motivation is often indicative of a lack of a compelling vision to pursue. Individuals that have an interesting vision are seldom unmotivated. While they may encounter failures and get upset or even moderately sad along the road, they tend to swiftly recover by reminding themselves of their goal.

Lack of drive is another indicator that you are not 'pursuing your joy.' It demonstrates a disconnect between your actions and who you are. The term 'enthusiastic' originates in Greek and meaning 'full with heavenly energy.' If you lack excitement, you are probably disconnected from your true self.

I've never heard of a noble prize laureate retiring early due to boredom. Indeed, the majority of them will continue to work until the day they die. This is because they have a well-defined objective. Likewise, I've never seen millionaires sell their businesses in order to retire to a tropical island. They may have attempted, but shortly discovered how monotonous their lives had become.

The idea is that you are not intrinsically unmotivated; you are just not doing what you are meant to do. You haven't pushed yourself far enough and haven't developed an inspiring vision. Perhaps you're locked in a never-ending cycle of boredom. Alternatively, you may be in your present position for financial gain or to satisfy your parents' expectations. Then it's unsurprising that you lack motivation. Fortunately, motivation may be regained.

How to develop via motivation (or a lack thereof)

A lack of drive indicates that you should create a life that is more consistent with who you are. It requires developing a thorough understanding of your abilities, personality, and preferences, while also ensuring that you use them on a daily basis.

How do you feel when you spend the majority of your day doing something you're bad at? Probably unmotivated. Regrettably, many individuals are trapped in professions that prevent them from using their skills. As a consequence, they continue to struggle and worry whether they will continue to suffer in the same manner for the next forty years. I've personally seen the difference between working at a job you hate and doing something you like. I can confirm that when you do what feels right to you, your level of drive and energy may be remarkable.

Have you ever noticed how you gravitate toward the things you excel at? While you may not love the activity itself, getting favorable comments instills pride in you and makes you feel good about yourself. Now, if you were continuously reminded of how inept you are at your work, would you still like it?

The idea is that there are things that you excel at and things that you love doing. Once you discover your strengths and devote as much time as possible to them, you will feel more driven. You may even discover that you appreciate jobs you never believed you would enjoy just because you are competent at them.

To concentrate on your skills, you may need to rewrite your present work description, switch roles within the same firm, or completely change careers. Remember, if every second of the day is a battle, you are probably not accomplishing your goals. You have strengths, and it is your responsibility to discover them.

Recognize your unique personality

This is slightly connected to the preceding point, since your personality plays a role in determining your abilities. For example, if you're an introvert, your work options will likely be different than if you're an extrovert. You may prefer to spend the majority of your time alone or in small groups and may avoid occupations that need constant interaction with customers. You could discover that you function better in a calm area.

Your basic values will also have an effect on your motivation level. Perhaps independence is critical to your well-being. If this is the case, self-employment may be preferable than a 9-to-5 job. Or maybe you thrive on novelty and want to continually learn. If this is the case, doing the same monotonous tasks may not provide you with any joy.

Recognize your motivations

Occasionally, you lack motivation because you establish a goal in an uninspiring manner. While the objective may be something you really want, the manner you define it or work toward it is just not compelling.

Assume you want to reduce weight. If none of the reasons for your goal emotionally connect with you, you will be unmotivated and will have a difficult time reaching it. Thus, your task is to ascertain the benefits of weight loss. Consider why you want to reduce weight. Continue to inquire why until you discover something that emotionally connects with you. Bear in mind that you seldom desire to lose weight just because it is the 'proper thing' to do. You want to reduce weight because it would improve your mood. This is the context in which you define weight loss, and it is critical that you get it right if you are to succeed.

Now, you may inquire as to why you are unable to reduce weight. It may assist you in determining the source of your difficulties. If you overeat to feel good, you should consider why. Is it a pattern? Is it as a result of your stress? Is it a result of your surroundings? Is it a means of evading something?

It is critical to understand why you are doing anything. Who knows what you can do if you have a compelling why?

Motivation is fickle

It's important noting here that you don't have to be motivated all the time. Motivation is fickle. There is no need to punish yourself if you are feeling uninspired. To assist you in acting when you lack motivation, it is critical to:

Have a strategy in place that enables you to remain on track with your objectives. Develop the self-discipline necessary to carry out tasks when you're not feeling it, and

Instead of blaming yourself for everything that goes wrong in your life, practice self-compassion and self-love.

Establishing a system is developing a daily routine that enables you to progress toward your objective. For instance, it may be dedicating a certain amount of time to a job first thing in the morning. Maintaining that routine on a daily basis is one approach to develop self-discipline. Another strategy is to create tiny daily objectives and regularly accomplish them. Self-compassion is encouraging yourself rather than condemning yourself.

To learn more about creating a morning routine, I recommend my book, Wake Up Call: How to Take Control of Your Morning and Transform Your Life.

Feeling imprisoned

At times, you may feel trapped. You are unmotivated to accomplish anything, or you are overwhelmed and are unsure why. This often occurs as a consequence of having too many open loops in your life or delaying on a significant assignment. Let us examine what you can do to free yourself.

A straightforward three-step procedure for resolving your impasse

Whenever you find yourself in a bind, attempt the following three-step procedure:

1. Create a list of all the tasks that must be completed.

2. Choose one chore that you have been putting off.

3. Complete the assigned assignment.

Often, there is one particular duty that you have been putting off for an extended period of time. While this may not be a challenging work, once you commit and do it, you will feel so happy that you will end up completing several other activities. As a consequence, you'll gain momentum and be able to break free. If you are unable to work on that particular activity, begin with a less frightening one. This will also assist you in gaining momentum.

If you've been deferring too many jobs or have an excessive number of incomplete projects, you may take the following steps:

1. Create a list of all the jobs or projects that need completion.

2. Allocate a set amount of time to accomplish them. Perhaps a few hours will enough to complete several of these activities. Or maybe you need further time. If this is the case, allow additional time.

3. For larger tasks, devote the next several days or weeks to completing just one.

4. Rearrange your calendar, assign some of your tasks, or forego some of your initiatives.

Conclusion

We appreciate your purchase of this book. My honest goal is that it helped you make sense of your feelings and equipped you with the skills necessary to begin regaining control. Bear in mind that the quality of your emotions is directly proportional to the quality of your life. As a result, understanding how to alter your behavior and surroundings in order to feel more pleasant emotions is critical to your wellness.

Let us be honest. You will continue to experience terrible feelings throughout your life, but ideally each time you will remember yourself that your emotions are not you and will learn to accept them in their current state before letting them go. You are not the one who is sad, depressed, jealous, or furious; you are the one who observes these feelings. You are what remains once these fleeting emotions vanish.

Your emotions are here to serve as a guide. Take all you can from them and then let go. Cling to them sparingly, as if your whole survival depended on them. That is not the case. Avoid associating with them as though they define you. They are not. Rather than that, utilize your emotions to propel you forward and remember that you are more than your feelings. How could you be otherwise? They will come and go, but you will remain. Always.

I'm looking forward to hearing from you! Your opinions and comments are valuable to me. I'd be quite thankful if you could provide a short review. Your help is very invaluable. I personally read every review in order to get your opinion and improve this book.

We appreciate your continued support!

www.ingramcontent.com/pod-product-compliance
Lightning Source LLC
Chambersburg PA
CBHW081720250726
48657CB00010B/3067